ZERO LIMITS

Breaking the Boundaries That Hold You Back

ELAINE ZELKER

Printed in the United States of America

Published in Hellertown, PA

Cover design by Christina Gaugler

Cover image by Serferis

Library of Congress Control Number 2023916819

ISBN 978-1-958711-74-3

For more information or to place bulk orders, contact the author or the publisher at Jennifer@BrightCommunications.net.

Mom and Dad,

This book is a testament to the legacy you left behind—a legacy of courage, perseverance, and unwavering love. It is a tribute to the values you instilled in me, which continue to shape my character and fuel my desire to make a positive impact on others. Your love is etched in my heart, an eternal flame that lights my path and keeps me connected to you, even in the silence.

See you on the other side,

Lainey

———

To Julia, Emily, and Kate,

Embrace your greatness, uniqueness, and talents with confidence. Know that there are zero limits to what you can achieve when you set your mind to it. Life might present challenges, but within you lies the power to conquer them all.

As you walk your path, never forget the value of gratitude, compassion, love, and kindness. Let these virtues be your compass in navigating the world with grace and purpose.

Always lift each other up, celebrate one another's victories, and be each other's biggest fans.

I am forever yours,

Momma

———

To Zeke,

Keep pushing me. I'm just getting started,

Elle

Contents

Introduction

Do you ever have the feeling that you're just coasting through life with no real sense of direction or purpose? Do you have lofty ambitions that seem unattainable? When it comes to finding a balance between work, family, and personal lives, many people confront difficulties. What if I told you that you have the ability within you to design a life that is meaningful, satisfying, and abundant? What if I told you that you could accomplish anything you put your mind to?

I know how tough it can be to juggle the demands of work and family because I've been in your shoes. A few years ago, I went through some major upheavals in my life, and I realized how precious and fleeting our time on this earth truly is. I knew that I had to do something that truly fulfilled me, something that I loved. That's when I took the leap and left my nursing career to pursue my passion for photography. After six years, I found myself shifting yet again. As much as I loved photography (and still do), I had a strong desire to provide greater value to those around me. In pursuit of this goal, I embarked on a journey of personal development, acquiring skills in goal setting, taking proactive measures, cultivating gratitude, and giving back to others.

I created my own personal mission statement with the help of a mentor. "To empower women to use their gifts and talents to rise and soar." Everything changed in my life. I now have purpose, and I'm driven by this mission. I have a clear vision. And I stay true to my own values.

It wasn't an easy road, and sometimes I doubted myself and wondered if I was making the right decision. Along the way, I learned a powerful lesson: If you're passionate about something and it aligns with your mission, vision, and values, you can accomplish anything. You can overcome any obstacle, no matter how daunting it might seem.

For the past 13 years, my entrepreneurial spirit has led me to many side hustles and businesses, including a thriving headshot photography business, co-owning multiple cafés along with a catering business, teaching and empowering other entrepreneurs, network marketing and sales, writing a few books, and spending lots of time on my DIY projects (which I sell on Etsy).

This book is designed to help new entrepreneurs or those looking to pivot and take on a new endeavor. (I wish I had this book 20 years ago!) It's specifically designed to empower women, especially those with multiple responsibilities, such as being a working parent or having a family. However, its valuable insights and practical advice can be beneficial for anyone who wants to take control of their life, unlock their true purpose, and accomplish their goals. I happen to be a mom to three daughters, so my perspective is a little more female-focused. Whether you're a woman navigating various roles or someone seeking guidance and support, this book offers valuable tools and inspiration for all readers.

You'll discover that you can do anything you're passionate about, as long as it aligns with your mission, vision, and values. You'll learn that it's not about following someone else's path or living up to someone else's expectations—it's about creating your own path, the one that is uniquely tailored to your passions, skills, and strengths.

Creating your own path can be scary, especially if you don't have the right tools and mindset (and the right people around you). I'm going to share with you the methods and strategies that have helped me build a successful business, achieve my goals, and create a life that is purposeful and fulfilling. You'll discover how to establish a strong sense of purpose and self-worth, set and achieve important objectives and goals, and cultivate gratitude.

Zero Limits will take you on a journey from A to Z, covering a wide range of topics that will empower you to create a life that has meaning and purpose and aligns with your gifts and talents. It's important to remember that I don't want you to feel overwhelmed. You can explore the content at a pace that feels comfortable and manageable for you. The goal is for you to have an enriching, enjoyable reading experience as you absorb the valuable insights and apply them to your life.

We'll start with the importance of accountability partners and how to find them. Then, we'll move on to facing your fears and overcoming obstacles. I'll show you how to write a mission statement that aligns with your values and passions and how to create an elevator pitch that captures the essence of who you are and what you do. Finally, we'll dive into the importance of challenging yourself, stepping out of your comfort zone, and embracing new opportunities. Throughout this journey, I'll share my personal experiences and the strategies that have helped me build a successful business and a fulfilling life. Along the way, I'll help you realize that there are ZERO LIMITS to what you can accomplish.

I also want to make something clear: Life is not always a straight path, and sometimes we need to pivot and adjust our course. I've done it multiple times in my life, and each time, it has led me to new and exciting opportunities.

So, let's do this together. Let's rise and soar and create a path that is uniquely tailored to your passions, skills, and strengths. It's time to take control of your life, discover your purpose, and achieve your goals. I'm here to be your guide, cheerleader, and accountability partner every step of the way. Let's get started.

A

ACCOUNTABILITY PARTNER

"Accountability breeds response-ability."—*Stephen R. Covey*

On the journey toward crushing our goals and aspirations, having a reliable support system can make all the difference in the world. Deep down, in the depths of our souls, we yearn for that unwavering support—the kind that resonates deep within our being. It's the longing for someone who will look us in the eye, place their hand on our shoulder, and say those magical words: "I've got your back." But not just empty words; rather, we need someone who genuinely means it. We need someone who will be there for us through thick and thin, in good times and bad, without a shadow of a doubt. That someone becomes your personal cheerleader, but also knows when to give you a loving kick in the pants when you need it and high-five you as you progress toward your goals.

So, what exactly is an accountability partner? An accountability partner is someone you choose who helps you stay accountable to your goals and commitments. They can provide real support, raw encouragement, and even the occasional tough love. Together, you share your goals, progress, and challenges regularly, and they hold you responsible for taking action toward achieving those goals.

Would My Spouse or Mom Make a Great Accountability Partner?

While it is possible for a spouse, child, or parent to serve as an accountability partner, there are a few factors to consider. In some cases, personal relationships with family members might be too emotionally involved or subjective, making it challenging to maintain an objective perspective when providing accountability. Additionally, there may be instances where the family dynamics or personal biases can interfere with the accountability process.

Ultimately, the choice of an accountability partner should prioritize a commitment to understanding your vision and goals, providing unbiased guidance, and holding you accountable for your actions. If you decide to choose a family member or someone beyond familiar boundaries, having a supportive and effective partnership can contribute significantly to personal growth and achievement.

Let's bring this to life with a real-life example. At a Chamber of Commerce event, Max and Abby found themselves engrossed in a conversation about their shared passion for writing. As they discussed their dreams of becoming authors, they discovered a commonality—they had both recently embarked on writing their first books. They know the challenges that lie ahead: self-doubt, procrastination, and the tempting urge to abandon their project. That's when they decided to team up and become each other's accountability partners, forging their path together.

Step one: They share their goals with each other.

Step two: They set up weekly meetups at a coffee shop or on Zoom, creating a dedicated space for their writing journey.

Step three: They become each other's accountability partners, setting weekly goals and writing targets to keep the creative fires burning.

Max and Abby eagerly await their weekly meetups, which become their platforms for exchanging feedback, brainstorming ideas, and supporting each other through the rollercoaster ride of the creative process. They celebrate every milestone achieved, whether it's completing chapters, reaching word count goals, or conquering pesky creative blocks. And when self-doubt rears its ugly head, one of them is quick to provide reassurance, reminding the other of their shared commitment, crushing that doubt once and for all.

Months later, Max and Abby proudly hold their manuscripts in their hands. They credit their accountability partnership for their remarkable achievements: the check-ins, the unwavering support, and their shared commitment to each other's goals. Not only do they feel more confident about themselves and their work, they've also developed a deep, lasting friendship built on a foundation of mutual support, understanding, and shared goals. It's a win-win situation. Their confidence grew. Their attention to time management and collaboration grew. They helped each other grow while building on each other's strengths and recognizing each other's weaknesses. They ended at a better place in terms of progress as compared to what they might have achieved alone.

Here's the exciting part: You don't have to stop at just one accountability partner. You can have multiple! Picture yourself with a team of accountability partners, united with you in the pursuit of crushing all your different goals. One partner can help you kick a bad habit, another to help you lose that "winter belly pooch," and yet another to support you on your journey to becoming a better boss, employee, or entrepreneur.

What Makes a Good Accountability Partner?

- **Brutal honesty:** A good accountability partner provides unfiltered, honest feedback.
- **Fearlessness:** They fearlessly address tough issues and challenge you when necessary.

- **Commitment:** They are fully invested in your growth and success.
- **Constructive criticism:** They offer feedback in a constructive manner, focusing on helping you improve.
- **Trustworthiness:** An accountability partner must be someone you trust implicitly.

How Do You Find an Accountability Partner?

Attend local networking events. It's like speed-dating for professionals! Get out there, mingle with like-minded individuals, and start forming relationships. Your local Chamber of Commerce is an excellent place to find out about events in your area.

Join professional organizations in your industry. You'll connect with knowledgeable individuals who share your interests and gain access to resources you might not have known existed.

Explore online communities. Seek out forums and groups in your sector or specialized field. Online forums, LinkedIn, and Facebook groups are treasure troves of potential accountability partners. If you can't find a group that suits you, why not create one yourself?

Attend workshops and seminars that align with your field of work. Not only will you pick up valuable knowledge, but you'll also have the chance to network with other like-minded individuals who are on their own journeys to success.

Don't be afraid to ask for recommendations. Reach out to friends, family, and coworkers for recommendations of businesses or individuals who might be interested in setting up an accountability partnership. Word-of-mouth can lead to incredible connections.

Utilize social media. Maybe you join a fitness group where you not only get the opportunity to share your personal milestones but join in the celebration of others' accomplishments. Use industry-specific hashtags to attract like-minded individuals who are also looking for accountability partners.

Create your own squad. If you can't find an accountability group that suits your needs, why not take the reins and create your own? Reach out to other business owners, extend an invitation, and form your own support system. Whether you gather in person or through online platforms, set objectives and maintain mutual accountability.

————

Personal Sidenote

I have the privilege of belonging to an accountability group called "The CEO Group," filled with badass female entrepreneurs. We're a dynamic bunch, typically ranging from six to eight members at any given time. The term "CEO" in our group stands for "Challenge Each Other," and boy, do we live up to that name! Our meetings are a melting pot of collaboration, where we share successes, failures, and everything in between. We work on ways to better ourselves and our teams by supporting each other in achieving our goals and staying true to our visions and missions. I can't emphasize enough the importance of prioritizing support instead of doing it alone.

We usually meet up every other month as a group (or take a quick "business" bus trip to NYC to shop and see a show). In between meet-ups, we meet individually as needed. I might call upon Ashley to help me manage my café staff. I may ask Kristine to help me launch a new event in one of our spaces. I could meet up with Lenore and ask her to share her experiences with the motivational guru she is working with to see how I can benefit from those nuggets. I chat with Tina about my PR needs and have her give me her honest feedback on how I'm presenting myself to the world. Every member has a different life story, skills, and experience to help one another navigate the unknown.

I am blessed to have my CEOs. They've got my back, even in my absence. They are my fearless partners, collaborators, and goal-getters. With their infectious energy and unwavering commitment, they push me to try new things, stay mission-driven, and soar to new heights.

Remember, when searching for accountability partners, look for those who share your values, passions, and goals. Seek out individuals who are committed to providing and receiving honest feedback and support. Don't settle for "yes, ma'am" partners; you want partners who will challenge you and help you grow. Set clear expectations and goals with your accountability partners to ensure that you're both working toward achieving your desired outcomes.

Creating your accountability network takes time and effort, but the rewards are immeasurable. With persistence, patience, and an open mind, you'll find yourself surrounded by encouraging, motivating people who will help you flourish.

Having an accountability partner offers numerous benefits for personal growth and goal achievement. They provide motivation, increase productivity, offer a fresh perspective, and give emotional support. Embrace the journey with your accountability partner(s) and enjoy the transformative impact they can have on your life.

B

BUILDING A STRONG FOUNDATION (FOR YOU AND
YOUR BRAND)

*"If you're not branding yourself, you can be sure others will do it for
you."—Unknown*

What Is a Brand?

In simple terms, a brand is the perception and reputation that
people have of a product, company, organization, *or individual.* It is
the overall image and identity associated with a particular entity. A
strong brand is one that is easily recognizable, trusted, and has a
positive reputation among its target audience.

Building a great brand foundation (whether for yourself or your
business) requires a combination of strategic planning, captivating
storytelling, and a deep understanding of your target audience's
needs and desires. Hold on to your hat, my friend, because we're
about to embark on a wild ride filled with laughter, lively verbiage,
and an abundance of delightful antics. ***I'm kidding!*** This chapter
might feel a little technical, but it's part of the process of taking your
personal (or business) brand from "meh" to marvelous!

Personal Brand vs. Business Brand

While a business brand and a personal brand share some similarities, there are important differences between them.

A business brand represents a company, organization, or product. It encompasses the values, mission, and image of the business. It focuses on establishing a reputation, building customer loyalty, and promoting products or services. A business brand is typically associated with a specific industry or market. For example, Apple is a well-known example of a business brand. Apple is associated with innovation, sleek design, and user-friendly technology products.

On the other hand, a personal brand revolves around an individual. It represents their unique skills, expertise, personalities, and values. A personal brand is about positioning oneself as an authority or thought leader in a particular niche. A personal brand can be applicable across various industries or areas of interest, like Elon Musk, the CEO of Tesla. His personal brand is built on qualities such as visionary thinking, entrepreneurship, and the pursuit of innovation.

You will see how personal and business brands intersect. I focus on the concept that "you are your brand" and explore how your personal values and beliefs can shape the values and mission of your business, infusing it with authenticity and purpose.

Your brand is not just a flashy logo and a catchy tagline. It's a reflection of your personal story—the essence of who you are and what you stand for. Think of it as the heartbeat of your business identity, pulsating with purpose, mission, vision, and values. These elements form the cornerstone of your brand, setting the stage for all future interactions. So, let's roll up our sleeves and get ready to build a strong brand foundation that accurately represents your image.

Building Your Brand Foundation

There are important elements that form a brand's foundation. You will find that the concepts of mission, vision, and values permeate throughout the pages of this book. These vital elements will be consistently emphasized, serving as the core focus of our discussions and insights.

Your mission: A mission (or mission statement) is a personal declaration that is particularly relevant to entrepreneurs. As an entrepreneur, your personal mission statement can serve as a guiding force for your business endeavors. It helps you define your purpose, goals, and values, which in turn shape the direction of your entrepreneurial ventures. The entirety of Chapter M is dedicated to crafting your own personal mission statement. You must uncover the purpose that drives your business and fuels your personal goals. Understanding this inspiration is key to creating a strong brand identity.

Your vision: A vision statement is also essential for charting the course for long-term success. It allows you to dream big and envision the future you aspire to create for yourself and your brand. To ensure consistency and integrity, defining your guiding beliefs and principles is essential. These serve as your compass, steering your decision-making process and inspiring you to think big. Chapter W —Wishes and Visions—will discuss this in great detail.

Your values: Finally, aligning your actions with your values and setting ambitious goals completes the foundation. Discovering how to embrace your core values enables you to create meaningful connections with your customers (and those around you), establishing trust and loyalty. We will explore practical strategies throughout this book for effectively communicating and showcasing your values, allowing your brand to resonate powerfully with your target market.

By integrating these key components, you establish an authentic, appealing brand that captivates your audience and paves the way for growth and success.

Building Your Brand's Story

Your brand's story and personality are the vehicles through which your purpose, mission, vision, and values are conveyed to your audience. When developing your brand's story and personality, consider the following.

- What is your brand's history and origin story? How did it all begin? Share the journey that led you to where you are today.
- What personality traits and characteristics represent your brand's identity? Are you bold and daring? Quirky and playful? Thoughtful and compassionate? Let your unique personality shine through.
- How can you showcase your brand's values and purpose through your story? Weave these elements into the fabric of your narrative, creating a cohesive, compelling brand story that captivates your audience.

The foundation of your brand's narrative is consistency. Ensure that your website, social media accounts, and marketing materials all embody the same brand story and personality. Presenting a consistent narrative across platforms strengthens your brand's identity and leaves a lasting impression.

Your brand's story is not just a mere recounting of events. It is an opportunity to combine your purpose, mission, vision, and values into a complete package. By crafting a compelling brand narrative, you will captivate your audience, foster meaningful connections, and pave the way for a brand that resonates deeply with those who encounter it.

Designing a Brand Identity

Your brand identity is the *visual* representation of your brand—the face that people see and remember. It includes your logo, color scheme, typography, and imagery. To design a memorable brand identity, consider the following.

- What emotions and feelings do you want to evoke in your audience? Think about the experiences you want them to have when they encounter your brand. Do you want them to feel inspired, empowered, or joyful?
- What colors, typography, and imagery best represent your brand's personality? Choose visuals that align with your brand's identity and resonate with your target audience.
- How can you use your brand's identity to tell your brand story? Infuse your brand's essence into every visual element, allowing your image to speak volumes about who you are and what you stand for.

If you need a little extra help, don't hesitate to work with a designer who can bring your vision to life. Together, you can create a unified brand identity that grabs attention and leaves a lasting impression.

Creating an Online Presence

In today's digital age, your online presence is the gateway to your brand. It's often the first point of interaction between you and your audience. So, let's ensure it leaves a lasting impression. Here are some action items to consider.

- Have a polished, professional-looking website that conveys the personality and message of your brand. Make sure it's user-friendly and reflects your brand's identity. Moreover, optimize your website for search engines by implementing SEO (Search Engine Optimization) strategies. Conduct thorough keyword research to identify relevant keywords and incorporate them naturally throughout your website's content. This will improve your website's visibility in search engine results, drive organic traffic, and increase your brand's online presence.

- Leverage social media platforms to actively engage with your audience, boost brand recognition, and build a community around your brand. Examples include Facebook, Instagram, Twitter, TikTok, and Pinterest.
- Create compelling, valuable content that showcases your expertise and positions you as a trusted authority in your industry. Share your knowledge and insights generously, whether through informative tutorials on YouTube, engaging videos on Instagram Stories and Reels, or thought-provoking blog posts on your website. By consistently delivering valuable content, you will cultivate trust, establish credibility, and solidify your reputation as a go-to resource in your field.
- Creating an email list and sending out regular newsletters helps keep your audience engaged and informed. You can create strong connections and provide valuable updates and insights that keep your audience invested in your brand.

Personal Sidenote

Let me share a little story with you—how my husband, Zeke, and I built our company, Zekraft—Curators of Taste. Now, imagine this: we decided to start this culinary journey right in the midst of the COVID lockdown. Crazy, right?

With tremendous talent and unwavering determination, Zeke decided to boldly undertake a monumental career shift after two decades as a filmmaker. He fearlessly dove into uncharted territories, following his passion for food. I watched my husband—a masterful filmmaker—stepping onto a new stage, ready to captivate tastebuds instead of audiences of moviegoers. The chaos of the world couldn't deter us from thinking big and pushing boundaries.

As we built Zekraft, we dedicated months to laying the foundation. From designing logos and creating style sheets to sourcing materials and finding the perfect packaging, every detail was meticulously crafted (no pun intended!). We wanted our brand to reflect our vision: to nourish our community with quick, healthful, locally sourced meals. However, it went beyond that. Our powerful mission states, "It's not simply about feeding or entertaining people, it's about nourishing them, body, mind, and spirit."

The process was a whirlwind, and in the midst of it all, I became my husband's biggest supporter, accountability partner, and cheerleader. We were in this together, 24/7. We hired a team that shared our vision and embraced our mission. Our brand had to be on point all the time, from the logo to training our staff. We knew that consistency across all our social media platforms, our website, and in person was essential. We couldn't hide behind curtains. We had to be present, authentic, and true to our brand's purpose.

Zekraft—Curators of Taste is not just a business; it's a reflection of our passion, resilience, and commitment to our community. In the heart of uncertainty, we found the courage to build something meaningful and impactful. Every interaction, meal, and act of generosity is an opportunity to make a positive difference.

With every challenge and triumph, we continue to remain dedicated to living our powerful mission of nourishing people—body, mind, and spirit. Our story is still unfolding, and we're excited to continue this journey of culinary delight and meaningful connections. Together with our team and the support of our community, we know that the future holds boundless opportunities for growth and success.

This is our brand.

C

COLLABORATION

"If you hang out with chickens, you're going to cluck, and if you hang out with eagles, you're going to fly."—*Steve Maraboli*

———

Collaborating can become one of the most important keys to unlocking your greatest business potential. Whether you're a small business owner, part of a huge corporation, a startup enthusiast, a direct sales guru, or a retiree pursuing a new hobby, one thing remains true: Collaborations are the lifeblood of growth. What does that mean exactly?

What *Is* Collaboration?

Collaboration (especially in the workplace) is what makes teamwork and goals successful. It's really that simple.

Collaboration is when a group of people come together and contribute their expertise for the benefit of a shared objective, project, goal or mission. It's like a photographer working with a makeup artist to create a cover image for a bridal magazine. In other words, collaboration is the process of *group work*. For some, it comes naturally, but for others, it's a learned skill, and how well you collaborate is equally important.

As my dad used to say, "It's not what you know; it's who you know and how you use it." The way to increase your "who" network is to put yourself out there and start collaborating.

Connections are key.

What Are the Benefits of Collaborating?

Collaborating can do several things.

Inspire you: Sometimes you have to think outside the box and try something new and innovative to grow. While reading and learning are important, actions will be more effective in your growth.

Help you gain confidence: The more you collaborate with others, the more confident you will become. Collaborating with others also brings different skill sets, perspectives, and strengths to the table, which will bring you more opportunities, which can inspire and motivate you.

Grow your circle: Put yourself out there and meet new people. Not only will expanding your network open doors to new opportunities, but it will also enrich your personal and professional growth through diverse perspectives and valuable connections

Save money: Get more bang for your buck by splitting responsibilities with fellow collaborators. Sharing expenses—such as a vendor table or booth—and doubling your marketing is a win-win situation.

It's important to follow a structured approach when collaborating.

Step One: Establish Clear Goals

What do you want to achieve by partnering with others? What are your business objectives?

Take a moment to envision what you hope to achieve by partnering with others. Are you seeking to expand your customer base, increase brand awareness, or explore new markets? Define your desired outcomes and consider how collaboration can help you attain them.

Furthermore, reflect on your comprehensive business objectives. What are the key milestones you aim to reach? Is it boosting revenue, enhancing product innovation, or improving operational efficiency? By aligning your collaborative efforts with these objectives, you ensure that every partnership and collective endeavor brings you closer to your ultimate vision.

Step Two: Identify Your Ideal Partners

These partners should possess the skills, experience, and resources necessary to help you achieve those goals. It is crucial to seek out individuals or organizations that align with your values and share a common vision, as this synergy forms the foundation for effective collaboration.

Imagine you are an aspiring chef with a deep passion for creating unique, healthy, and innovative culinary experiences. Your dream is to establish a gourmet restaurant that showcases farm-to-table cuisine, blending flavors from diverse culinary traditions.

To bring this vision to life, you recognize the importance of finding partners who can complement your skills and contribute to the success of your venture. In your exploration, you happen upon a local farm known for its organic, sustainable produce. You see a perfect fit between their dedication to moral farming practices and your goal of providing farm-to-table dining experiences.

Although you might not be acquainted with the farm's owners initially, their dedication to quality and sustainability resonates deeply with your vision. You *reach out* to start a conversation because you are interested in the possibility of working together.

As you dive into discussions, you uncover shared values and a mutual passion for showcasing the best that nature has to offer. By joining forces, you can establish a direct supply chain, ensuring the freshest, finest ingredients for your meal creations. Collaborating with the farm allows you to feature seasonal and locally sourced produce, elevating the farm-to-table experience at your restaurant to new heights. Moreover, this partnership enables you to contribute to the sustainable food movement while delighting your customers with innovative, memorable dishes.

This is pretty much the story of Zekraft, as we vend at a few local farmer's markets and source our lettuces, fruits, veggies, and more from our local farmers. We have established long-lasting, genuine relationships because they are in alignment with our own mission, vision, and values.

Remember, collaborating often involves stepping beyond your familiar circles and engaging with individuals who possess the expertise and resources you seek. Embrace the opportunity to connect with partners who share your passion and values, even if they are initially unfamiliar to you.

Step Three: Execute Your Collaboration Effectively

This means establishing clear roles and responsibilities, communicating with your partners and measuring your progress toward your goals. It's important to talk about deadlines and delegate tasks at this point. At Zekraft, when we collaborate with others, we make sure our cost of goods makes sense, our margins are manageable, and our quality and standards are discussed ahead of time. For example, every piece of lettuce is inspected by the farmer and our staff at Zekraft, delivery and packaging terms are discussed ahead of time, and all kinks are ironed out as we establish our relationship.

Here are a few more examples.

- A photographer hosts a wedding vendor event at their studio and invites local florists, videographers, caterers, bakers, and makeup artists to attend. The photographer benefits by having access to a variety of potential clients, and the other vendors benefit by being able to showcase their work and potentially gain new customers.

- A coffee shop invites new local artists to showcase their work every other month. The coffee shop benefits by having new, interesting artwork on display, which can attract customers. The artists benefit by having a space to showcase their work and potentially gain new customers and make sales!
- Someone in direct sales organizes an online vendor fair, featuring several other online companies. This allows them to showcase their products and services to a wider audience and potentially gain new customers. By collaborating, network marketers can leverage each other's networks and resources to achieve better results.

These are situations where *both parties* involved benefit from the partnership.

Finally, don't forget about your local Chamber of Commerce, small business networks, Polka Dot Powerhouses, Toastmasters, and BNI. These organizations are designed to facilitate collaboration and networking between businesses. By joining these organizations, you can gain access to a wider network of potential partners and customers.

In conclusion, collaboration is a valuable tool that can help entrepreneurs unlock their business potential and achieve greater success. By working with others who share your vision and values, you can leverage each other's strengths and resources to achieve more than you could on your own. The benefits of collaboration are numerous, including increased creativity, access to resources, shared risks and rewards, improved learning, and enhanced visibility.

As Helen Keller said, "Alone we can do so little; together we can do so much."

Personal Sidenote

You might have guessed, but most of the above examples are collaboration stories from my own life. Collaboration is truly key to success in the world of business, and joining a network of like-minded individuals can make a world of difference. For instance, I joined my local Polka Dot Powerhouse (located in the Lehigh Valley area of Pennsylvania) in January 2023. The experience has been inspiring, as I'm constantly surrounded by other like-minded, motivated women entrepreneurs and great individuals. By collaborating with some of the members, I've expanded my reach and grown my business in ways that I couldn't have done alone. Thanks to these collaborations, I'm now on more advisory boards, booking more speaking engagements, and even helping others launch their own small businesses by selling their products in our cafés. I've realized that the opportunities are endless when it comes to collaboration and that it's important to always keep an eye out for ways to partner with others who share your vision and values. It's helped broaden my network and create long-lasting relationships. I'm excited to continue to hunt for opportunities, build meaningful partnerships that drive results, and encourage you to do the same.

D

DISTINCTIVELY DIFFERENT

"Fitting in allows you to blend in with everyone else, but being different allows you to be yourself, to be unique, and to be more creative."—*Sonya Parker*

In today's bustling marketplace, setting yourself apart and standing out is paramount to achieving success. Take a moment to stroll down any city street—how many pizza places or cafés do you encounter? And yet, among the multitude of options, why do some establishments capture the spotlight while others fade into the background?

While delivering a quality product or service is essential, it is equally vital to carve out your own unique identity amidst the competition. You don't have to start from scratch or reinvent the wheel. By infusing a touch of individuality into what you already do, while staying true to your mission, vision, and values, you can unlock the power of differentiation.

In this chapter, we will explore actionable strategies to help you embrace your distinctiveness and stand out in the crowd. From understanding your competitors to leveraging your strengths and measuring your success, these tips will guide you on the path to becoming distinctly different.

Know Your Competitors

Before you can differentiate yourself from your competitors, you need to know who they are and what they offer. Here are some ways to research your competitors.

- **Google search**: Begin your quest with a Google search tailored to your industry or niche. Watch as the search results unfold before your eyes, revealing a lineup of similar businesses. Explore their websites and immerse yourself in their marketing materials. Observe how they position themselves in the marketplace. Start with the most prominent players, check out how they operate, and then look more closely in your own local area.
- **Social media**: Explore your competitors' social media profiles and observe their posts. Pay attention to their language, visuals, hashtags, and messaging. Take note of their interactions with customers. Do they conduct giveaways or contests? Are they responsive to inquiries and engaged with their audience?
- **Customer reviews**: Read customer reviews of your competitors to gain insights into what people like or dislike about their products or services. These reviews will provide valuable intelligence to help understand their strengths and weaknesses. Customer reviews can be an invaluable resource for understanding what people appreciate or disapprove of your competitors' products or services. By reading these reviews, you can gain insights into their strengths and weaknesses. However, it's important to be cautious of inauthentic reviews that might not accurately reflect genuine customer experiences. Always consider the overall consensus and look for patterns in the feedback to make informed assessments.

Now that you have gained insights into your competitors, it's time to carve out a distinct space for your brand. Here are effective strategies for successful differentiation.

Embrace your unique qualities. Reflect on what sets your brand apart. What makes you/your business truly unique? Identify the distinct qualities that define your brand and make it stand out. Write down these unique attributes and ensure they align with your original mission and vision.

Highlight your strengths. Capitalize on your strengths as a business or individual to create a compelling narrative. Highlighting these strengths will further differentiate you and your brand. Consider the following examples to accentuate your unique selling points in your marketing:

- **Exceptional expertise**: If you possess specialized knowledge or skills, emphasize them. Showcase your qualifications, certifications, and experience. Share insightful content that positions you as an expert in your field. *"As a certified nutritionist with more than a decade of experience, I provide personalized meal plans and evidence-based advice that helps clients achieve their health goals."*
- **Unparalleled quality:** If your products or services excel in quality, emphasize the meticulous attention to detail, superior craftsmanship, or the use of premium materials. Leverage customer testimonials and reviews that emphasize the outstanding quality you provide. *"Our handcrafted leather bags are meticulously crafted using the finest Italian leather, ensuring durability and timeless elegance that surpass industry standards."*
- **Innovative approaches:** If your brand thrives on innovation, highlight the unique solutions, cutting-edge technology, or forward-thinking strategies you employ. Showcase how your approach sets you apart and relieves customer pain points in ways that others cannot. *"At our café, we have revolutionized the traditional coffee experience with our state-*

of-the-art brewing techniques, such as nitrogen-infused cold brew and pour-over methods that unlock new flavors and aromas."

- **Stellar customer service:** If your customer service is exceptional, make it a key selling point. Emphasize the personalized care, prompt responsiveness, and proactive measures you take to ensure customer satisfaction. Showcase customer testimonials that speak to the remarkable service experience you provide. *"Our dedicated support team is available 24/7 to provide prompt assistance and resolve any concerns, ensuring our customers receive exceptional service at every touchpoint."*

Instead of just telling your audience how you're different, show them. Use visuals, customer testimonials, and examples to demonstrate your unique qualities.

Remember, your unique qualities and strengths form the foundation of your differentiation strategy. By leveraging these attributes and aligning them with your mission and vision, you can position your business as distinctive and compelling. Let your distinctiveness shine through in all aspects of your marketing to attract and retain loyal customers.

Measure Your Success

Now, let's dive into the "tech-y" side of things and measure the success of your distinctively different approach. It's crucial to assess whether your efforts are yielding the desired results. Here are some methods to measure your progress.

Track website traffic. Harness the power of tools like Google Analytics to track and analyze your website traffic. Determine if your marketing endeavors are successfully driving an increased number of visitors to your site.

Measure social media engagement. Keep a watchful eye on your social media profiles and assess the engagement metrics. Monitor the monthly likes, comments, and shares your posts receive.

This provides insights into the level of audience engagement with your distinct content.

Observe customer reviews. Track customer reviews meticulously. Take note of whether people are mentioning your unique qualities and what sets you apart from your competitors. These candid opinions can guide you in evaluating the impact of your distinctiveness.

Survey your audience. Conduct surveys to dive into the perceptions of your business. Seek to understand whether people perceive your brand as distinctively different. This valuable feedback illuminates the effectiveness of your differentiation strategy.

Success Story

Sophia, a skilled and passionate barber, set out on her entrepreneurial journey and opened a barbershop in a vibrant neighborhood known for its diverse range of businesses (and many other barbershops).

Determined to create an exceptional experience for her clients, she aims to differentiate her barbershop from the competition. In addition to amazing haircuts, Sophia offers specialized services and treatments that are uncommon in other barbershops, including hot towel shaves, beard grooming consultations, scalp massages, and personalized styling advice.

How did she begin?

Research competitors. Sophia conducted extensive research on existing barbershops in the area. She visited their physical locations, explored their websites, and examined their social media presence. Through her research, she realized that most barbershops offer traditional services without a unique touch. She noticed a lack of attention to detail and personalized experiences, leaving customers longing for more.

Embrace unique qualities. Sophia identified her barbershop's unique qualities and aligns them with her vision. She decided to focus on creating a welcoming, inclusive atmosphere where clients receive exceptional haircuts and also enjoy a customized styling experience tailored to their preferences. She envisioned her shop as a haven that celebrates individuality and fosters connections with her clients. She engages with them, gets to know them, and hosts events to foster camaraderie between her staff and clients.

Highlight strengths. Recognizing her strengths as a talented barber, Sophia highlights her expertise and dedication to her craft. She offers specialized services, such as intricate hair designs and personalized consultations, ensuring that each client receives a unique, tailored experience. Sophia's shop also is known for providing a warm, friendly environment where clients feel comfortable expressing their style preferences and engaging in conversations with other barbers and customers.

Measure success. To gauge the success of her distinctiveness, Sophia implemented several effective measurement methods:

- Tracking client traffic. Sophia keeps track of the number of clients who visit her shop, allowing her to observe trends and determine whether her unique approach is attracting more clients over time.
- Monitoring social media engagement. Sophia actively manages her shop's social media profiles to engage with her clients and showcase her skills. She encourages clients to share their before-and-after transformations, and she actively responds to comments and messages. The growing number of followers, likes, and positive engagement demonstrates the increasing interest and satisfaction of Sophia's clients.
- Assessing client reviews and feedback. Sophia pays close attention to client reviews and feedback, eagerly listening to their experiences and preferences. Positive reviews mentioning the personalized styling experience, exceptional attention to detail, and friendly atmosphere validate her unique qualities and reinforce her commitment to client satisfaction.

- Conducting satisfaction surveys: Sophia periodically conducts satisfaction surveys to gather feedback from her clients, seeking their perceptions of her shop's distinctiveness. The survey results consistently reveal high satisfaction levels, showcasing her ability to create an extraordinary grooming experience that sets her apart from her competition.

Through Sophia's efforts to be distinctively different, her barbershop became a space for clients seeking an exceptional styling experience. By leveraging her unique qualities, showcasing her expertise, and consistently measuring her success, Sophia successfully sets her shop apart from competitors, establishing a loyal clientele that appreciates her commitment to personalized care.

E

EMPOWERMENT

"Never bend your head. Always hold it high. Look the world straight in the eye."—Helen Keller

———

What does *empowerment* mean to you?

The dictionary says it is the "authority or power given to someone to do something," or "the process of becoming stronger and more confident, especially in controlling one's life and claiming one's rights."

Empowerment is quite simple. It's about choices: Choosing to go down one road or another. Choosing to change careers or not. Choosing to marry or stay single. The *power* from empowerment comes in the active choices you make to live the life you want.

This is why my personal mission statement proclaims: To empower women to use their gifts and talents to rise and soar. Empowerment goes beyond waiting for others to meet your needs; it emboldens you to seize control, shaping your own destiny. It is the fuel that propels you forward, nurturing a growth mindset, fostering self-trust, and harnessing your innate abilities to achieve greatness. Empowerment is not merely a style of thinking; it is a way of living that leads you to conquer obstacles, embrace challenges, and construct a life that is rich with meaning and fulfillment.

The following six steps will equip you with the tools to motivate and uplift both yourself and others. You will be armed with all the ammunition needed to showcase to the world the extraordinary sense of your being.

Step One: Believe in Yourself

The first step on this empowering journey is to believe in yourself 100 percent. You hold the reins of your destiny, and it's time to embrace your true potential. Take a moment to acknowledge your unique strengths, talents, and abilities. These are the building blocks of your success.

Now, envision a future brimming with endless possibilities. Set daring goals that spark a fire within you and push the boundaries of what you previously thought possible. Let your goals serve as catalysts for personal growth, propelling you toward new horizons. As you embark on this transformative path, surround yourself with positive, like-minded individuals who uplift and believe in your dreams. Leave the skeptics and naysayers behind. They are not your people.

Tap into the source of self-belief that resides deep within you. Allow it to fuel your every action, propelling you toward greatness. In this journey of self-empowerment, you are your number one fan. Champion yourself, be your own cheerleader, celebrate your victories, and embrace the challenges as stepping stones to your ultimate success.

Step Two: Cultivate a Growth Mindset

A growth mindset is characterized by the belief that abilities, intelligence, and talents can be developed (learned) and improved through dedication, effort (action), and perseverance (never giving up). It is the understanding that one's potential is not fixed or predetermined, but rather malleable and expandable. Individuals with a growth mindset embrace challenges, view failure as an opportunity for learning and growth, and are open to new experiences and possibilities.

A growth mindset is essential for empowerment. It's about seeing challenges as opportunities to learn and grow rather than as obstacles. When you have a growth mindset, you're willing to take risks, try new things, and learn from your mistakes. We will cover overcoming fear and failure in the next chapter. Cultivating a growth mindset is also about surrounding yourself with people who inspire and challenge you. Perhaps you can read more books that broaden your horizons or take courses that expand your knowledge and look for ways to invest in your mind and yourself. Engage with a community of curious minds that encourages you to stretch your limits and explore new possibilities.

Step Three: Break the Chains of Limiting Beliefs

You deserve to live the life you truly desire. Period.

Limiting beliefs are like invisible chains that restrain you, stop your progress, and prevent you from reaching your goals. They come from your own negative self-talk and past experiences that have shaped your perception of yourself and your abilities. Let's be truthful. You have the power to conquer them, shatter them into a million pieces, and redefine what is possible for you. To embark on this freeing path of overcoming limiting beliefs, you must first challenge them head-on. Take a bold stand against the voice that whispers:

"You can't do this."

"You suck."

"You're not good enough!"

Replace it with a resounding affirmation that declares:

"I am capable and will figure this out."

"I am prepared to open my own business."

"I am excited to speak in front of this huge crowd."

"I studied so hard; I'm going to ace this exam."

Embrace the belief that with determination, effort, and a growth mindset, you can conquer any obstacle that stands in your way.

Step Four: Take Action

Belief and mindset lay a sturdy foundation, but true transformation emerges from *taking action*.

Empowerment is not a passive endeavor; it demands the courage to step out of your comfort zone and proactively shape your destiny. Thinking about it is not enough. You must embark on a journey of deliberate action to breathe life into your aspirations.

Begin by setting your sights on small, attainable goals—the stepping stones that lead to the fulfillment of your larger dreams. With each step forward, you ignite a spark of momentum that propels you closer to your desired destination. Celebrate even the smallest victories along the way, savoring the sweet taste of accomplishment, and allowing them to fuel your determination to persist.

No matter how insignificant it might seem, every action you take acts as a link between the world of possibilities and the world of reality. Every step you take forward gives your journey meaning and moves you closer to realizing your dreams. You will become more empowered every step of the way.

Step Five: Collaborate with Other Empowered People

Empowerment is contagious, and when you surround yourself with supportive people, you'll be inspired to become more empowered yourself. Seek mentors, coaches, and like-minded individuals who share your values and vision. Join networking groups and attend events where you can connect with other encouraging people. Together, you can support and uplift each other on your journeys to success.

Step Six: Empower Others

True empowerment reaches its pinnacle when we extend a helping hand to uplift and inspire others. As we share our knowledge, skills, and experiences, we become catalysts for their growth and success. Look for opportunities to mentor or coach people who are embarking on their own transformative journeys, offering guidance, support, and encouragement. Celebrate their achievements and provide unwavering assistance during challenging times. By empowering others, we create a ripple effect of positivity and inspiration that has the power to change lives and shape a better world.

When we empower others, we amplify their potential, and we also cultivate a legacy of transformation. Each person we uplift becomes a torchbearer, passing on the gift of empowerment to others. By embracing this responsibility, we contribute to a collective tapestry of growth, resilience, and achievement. Let us unite in the mission to create a society where empowerment becomes the norm, where every individual is empowered to rise, soar, and make a meaningful impact. Together, we can forge a future where the power of empowerment knows no bounds.

———

Personal Sidenote

Empowerment is not just a word to me; it's a way of life and a guiding principle that shapes everything I do. I believe that everyone has the potential to rise and soar and to use their unique gifts and talents to create a fulfilling, meaningful existence. That's why my mission is to empower as many people as I can, to inspire them to believe in themselves, and to take ownership of their lives. If I could add one more tattoo to my body, it would be my mission statement (the shorter version): To empower women to use their gifts and talents to rise and soar! (It's a tad long though, so if you're a graphic artist and want to mock something up for me, hit me up at info@elainezelker.com.)

I live and breathe this mission every day, and it's the driving force behind everything I do. Whether I'm coaching someone to overcome their limiting beliefs, writing a book on empowerment, or simply greeting each morning with love and gratitude in my heart, I know that I'm making a difference in the world.

My former business coach once told me that her goal was to help 1,000 people help 1,000 people, and that has inspired me. I know that I'm a part of her 1,000, and now you are a part of mine. I feel a deep sense of obligation to follow her mission as well as my own. I have become the torchbearer. I surround myself with like-minded people, and I've learned to say goodbye to the toxicity in my life. I know that by surrounding myself with positivity and inspiration, I'm better able to live out my mission and inspire others to do the same. Whether it's taking a leap of faith to write this book, creating an amazing headshot, or seeing my baristas interact with customers in a loving, caring manner, every action I take empowers me and those around me.

Set a daily goal for yourself to encourage at least one person. As you do this, it will become a habit, and supporting others will become second nature. Empowerment is about taking ownership of your life and using your gifts and talents to create a meaningful, fulfilling existence.

Empowerment is not a one-time event, but a journey that requires ongoing dedication and commitment. Stay focused on your goals, seek out support and inspiration when you need it, and never give up on your dreams. With hard work and determination, you can become the empowered person you were meant to be and inspire others to do the same. Rise and soar, my friend!

F

FACING YOUR FEARS

"F-E-A-R has two meanings: 'Forget Everything And Run' or 'Face Everything And Rise.' The choice is yours."—Zig Ziglar

When you begin your journey, or experience even a change in your current situation, you might feel excited, yet intimidated. You may have these grand ideas but freeze up before taking the first step. Inevitably, fear creeps in, stopping you from taking crucial steps toward your aspirations and dreams. It is important not to allow fear to become an obstacle. By embracing a proactive approach, you can overcome fear and enable the confident pursuit of your passion. This life-changing process begins with consciously acknowledging your fears, followed by a mental reconfiguration to perceive them as a challenge rather than a hindrance and develop some grit. How? Start with these five steps.

Step One: Admit You're Afraid

Be upfront with yourself. The first step in conquering your fears is admitting that you have them. In a journal, describe your fears in detail and write how they are preventing you from moving forward. The fear of failing, of being rejected, or of falling short of one's own ideals are all examples of such fears. The act of putting your worries on paper is the first step in coming to terms with them. By looking them straight in the eye, eventually, you will be able to let them all go.

In the pursuit of conquering your fears, the first step toward liberation is boldly acknowledging their presence by literally saying, "Hello, fear."

It's time to have an honest conversation with yourself, diving into the details of these apprehensions. Grab your journal and start writing. Paint a vivid picture of the fears that cling to your thoughts, those barriers that have hindered your progress. Whether it's the fear of failure, the dread of rejection, or the nagging worry of falling short of your own ideals, capture them boldly in written form.

Examples:

"What if I don't finish the project?"

"What if no one comes to my opening?"

"So many other people have Etsy shops. Why would someone buy from me?"

By directly confronting these fears and seeing them through your own words, you kickstart the process of diminishing their influence. Look them square in the eye, fearless and unyielding. It's through this act of bold confrontation that their hold on your aspirations will gradually loosen. As you pour your fears onto the page, you'll discover the strength and clarity needed to let them go, liberating yourself to pursue your passion with determination.

Step Two: Rethink Your Fear

How would your perspective shift if the concept of failure was eliminated? Would you approach situations with a renewed sense of confidence and determination? It's likely. So let's begin cultivating that mindset. Rewrite the script in your mind, replacing doubts and apprehensions with positive reinforcements.

"I know this will be scary, but I'm so ready!"

"My knees are shaking, but I'm prepared to speak on that stage now."

"Deep breaths. I got this! I've had great mentors. I'll make some mistakes; however, I'll learn from them and move on!"

Embrace the belief that success is within your reach and let this empowering outlook guide your actions and decisions. By reformatting the words in your own mind, you pave the way for a mindset that thrives on possibility and propels you toward achieving your goals.

Step Three: Pursue What Truly Excites You

Have you ever experienced that moment when someone's eyes sparkle with enthusiasm as they discuss something they truly love? It's a powerful reminder that fear can indeed be conquered through the power of passion. By directing your energy toward something that sets your soul on fire, you can squash your fears and achieve remarkable things.

Take a moment to reflect on the driving force behind starting your own venture. What inspired that initial spark? Now, go a little deeper and explore your deepest passions. Consider the activities that ignite an uncontainable excitement within you—those pursuits that keep your spirits high and your determination unwavering. And remember, your passion doesn't have to be limited to your current line of work. It might lie hidden within a unique talent or a cherished hobby. Once you have identified what truly matters to you, embrace it wholeheartedly as your secret weapon against fear. As you pursue what excites you most, you'll find yourself radiating with a newfound courage, ready to conquer any obstacle that stands in your way. Go all in. On the one side, you'll have fear, weighing you down, while on the other side, you'll find passion, bringing out a rise within you. All you have to do is take that leap of faith and jump.

Step Four: Prepare Yourself

Building resilience—the ability to bounce back from adversity—is an asset in your quest to conquer fear. Here are some effective strategies to cultivate resilience.

Prioritize self-care. To maintain your strength and focus, it's crucial to take care of yourself both emotionally and physically. Engage in activities that nourish your well-being, such as exercising regularly, getting enough sleep, eating a balanced diet, and practicing mindfulness or relaxation techniques. By tending to your own needs, you'll enhance your ability to overcome challenges.

Seek supportive allies. Surround yourself with like-minded individuals who share your goals and values. These allies will cheer you on and also provide constructive feedback and guidance when needed. A supportive network can bolster your resilience, while offering different perspectives and helping you stay motivated during tough times.

Stay focused on your goals. In the face of setbacks and obstacles, it's essential to maintain unwavering determination and perseverance. Keep your eye on the prize, reminding yourself of the ultimate outcome you desire. Set clear, achievable goals and develop a plan to reach them. Even when faced with adversity, stay committed to your goals and adapt your strategies as necessary. Remember, setbacks are just temporary roadblocks on the path to success.

Armed with resilience, you're ready to face whatever challenges come your way. Embrace this mindset, take action, and start swinging toward your goals. Resilience is a skill that can be developed and strengthened over time, so keep pushing forward with determination and a fighting spirit.

Step Five: Take Action

When it comes to calming your nerves, taking action is a powerful tactic. Begin by tackling manageable tasks and gradually progress to more challenging ones. For example, if the thought of delivering a speech to a large audience makes you jittery (and, let's be honest, it does to most of us), start by practicing in front of a mirror or with a trusted partner. Gradually expand your comfort zone by presenting to a smaller audience, like close friends or coworkers. Remember to acknowledge and celebrate every step of your progress along the way.

By diving into action, you confront your fears head-on and also build confidence through practical experience. Each step you take, no matter how small, is a testament to your courage and growth. So push through the initial nerves, embrace the opportunity to learn and improve, and revel in the satisfaction of your achievements.

Greatness is often created in moments of discomfort. By embracing action and persisting through your apprehensions, you unlock your true potential and pave the way for personal and professional growth. So move *fear-ward*, take that first step, and let your actions become the catalysts for your success. You are worthy of that!

———

Personal Sidenote

I don't often tell this story, but I'm going to share it with you. In the early 2000s, I lost both of my parents and then got divorced. I had three little girls. I went down to about 95 pounds, moved into a townhouse, began joint custody, and lived by myself for the first time in my entire life. Fear crippled me. It had me sitting in a tub one lonely night after drinking a bottle of wine, contemplating my life.

Why am I here?

What if I was not here?

I was questioning everything. I had a career with some heavy-duty golden handcuffs—great salary and great perks—but no passion. No fire. Just existing. Living the life my parents and ex-husband wanted me to (or so I thought). I plastered on a fake smile and just coasted by.

That was rock bottom for me, and my ah-ha moment. I knew something had to change. I had to change my mindset. I told myself to put on my big girl panties, "Buck up Buttercup," and get ready to go balls-to-the-wall. I would not allow fear to take over. Where was that little resilient Italian tomboy who used to play tackle football with the boys growing up without a care in the world? She's still right here.

Backstory: I took a black-and-white film photography class at Rutgers University and loved it. Back in the early 1990s, women couldn't be artists, or at least that was what I was told. So I finished up my psych degree, then went to nursing school and became an RN. Don't get me wrong; I loved being a nurse. I did so much with it. I helped run a dermatology practice, was an EMT, worked in numerous specialties, and ended my career in hospice nursing. All along, I still loved the camera and took a gazillion photos of my kids. (Something my dad did his whole life with us.)

I met my second husband, Zeke (the best accountability partner and cheerleader around), and with some encouragement, picked up the camera again, and when I did this, my heart raced. And I decided to go all in. I had massive *fear* on one side, and a fireball of *passion* on the other, and I took the leap. I admit: I was afraid. I journaled, went to yoga, meditated, you name it. I then had to rethink my fear. Was it real or imaginative? I looked at my fear as an opportunity to learn a new trade. I began to see myself as a photographer. I began to think about the success it could bring me and my family. I was excited about something again. I was truly passionate about capturing special moments for people in their happy times, memories that would last a lifetime. I put my gloves on and fought my way through the naysayers and Debbie Downers who said:

"You're doing what?"

"You can't do that; you have a job."

"You're crazy; you have three kids!"

Well, guess what? I took action and did it. I planned my exit from nursing and upped my game in photography. I found a mentor and learned from the best in the country. During this transition, I combined my nursing with photography and published my first book, *The Hand-Some Journey: Portraits of Elders Reflecting on Their Life Journeys*, which focused on hospice patients holding the one object that represented their life journey. My first subject held a martini glass!

I had a major fear, but I allowed my passion to outweigh it and took the leap of faith. Fifteen years later, I'm a serial entrepreneur, head-shot photographer, café owner, author, speaker, crafter, proud momma, wife, friend, and lover of life.

It's okay to seek help or support from professionals if fear or anxiety becomes overwhelming or debilitating. I personally sought the help of a therapist when I was struggling with my own fears and anxieties during my darker days. With the guidance and support of my therapist and loving, supportive family, I was able to work through my fears and develop the tools and resilience needed to pursue my passions with confidence. Don't hesitate to seek help if you need it. It's a sign of strength, not weakness.

G

GRATITUDE, GROWTH, AND GIVING BACK

"This is a wonderful day. I have never seen this one before."—Maya Angelou

———

Have you ever looked around and noticed just how many people are struggling to find their way, desperately searching for that mix of fulfillment and success? It seems like everywhere you turn, people are convinced that achieving monumental goals or swimming in a pool of cash will be the golden ticket to eternal happiness. Let me drop a truth bomb on you: They're missing three crucial ingredients: gratitude, growth, and giving back.

Picture a life where you appreciate the good things that come your way and actively cultivate a deep sense of gratitude for every twist and turn, stumble, and victory. That's where the magic happens. It's about embracing that attitude of awe and appreciation for the simple joys and extraordinary moments that fill our lives because, let's face it: Life's not just about chasing after dreams. It's about savoring the journey and being grateful for every step along the way.

Don't forget about your own personal growth. Imagine expanding your horizons, pushing boundaries, and discovering new facets of yourself that you never knew existed. It's like embarking on an adventure within your own soul, where every challenge becomes an opportunity for growth and every setback is a chance to bounce back stronger than ever before.

Now, for the best part: giving back. It's about the joy that comes from spreading kindness, making a positive impact, and leaving the world a little brighter than you found it. Whether it's helping someone going through a rough time, supporting a cause close to your heart, or simply sharing a smile with a stranger, the act of giving back benefits others and also nourishes your own soul.

By incorporating gratitude, growth, and giving back into your life, you'll be able to create a life that's fulfilling and successful and also filled with joy, purpose, and a whole lot of fun.

Here are some strategies I employ.

Gratitude: The Attitude of Abundance

Gratitude is the very foundation of a truly fulfilling life. It's all too common to find ourselves fixating on what we lack or stress about the challenges that come our way. Let me ask you this: Isn't that just plain exhausting? The comparison. The judgement. The "keeping up with the Joneses." I've been there, and I know how draining it can be. Let me share some powerful insights on how practicing gratitude can shift your mindset toward abundance.

When you shift your focus to what you already have, no matter how big or small, you start attracting more of the same. By doing so, you cultivate a mindset of abundance and contentment. It's about recognizing the positive aspects of our lives and being open to receiving more blessings, opportunities, and positive experiences. It's like a cosmic magnet that pulls in positivity and goodness. Gratitude is a force to be reckoned with. It has the power to transform our lives in countless ways, opening up new opportunities and bringing joy into every corner of our existence.

Now, let's explore some practical tips for cultivating gratitude, some tried-and-true strategies that can make a world of difference in your daily life.

Keep a gratitude journal. (We'll do a deeper dive into this in Chapter J.) Every morning or evening, write three things you are grateful for. If you're so inclined, keep writing. They can be big or small; it doesn't matter. The act of writing them down and reflecting on them will help shift your mindset to one of abundance. Dig deep and go beyond the basic stuff you see around you.

Some examples:

"I am grateful for my morning coffee."

"I am grateful for the sound of my kids laughing."

"I am grateful for my comfortable bed."

Dig deeper:

"I'm thankful for the laughter shared with friends last night. It reminded me of the power of connection and how it uplifts my spirit."

"Today, I'm grateful for the challenges I faced in my personal life. They have taught me resilience and the ability to overcome adversity, making me stronger and more determined."

"Today, I'm grateful for the opportunity to learn something new. Whether it's through a book, a podcast, or a conversation, I embrace the chance to expand my knowledge and broaden my horizons."

Practice gratitude throughout the day. Make it a habit to express gratitude for the good things that happen to you during the day. Did someone hold a door open for you? Did you enjoy a delicious cup of coffee? Did you have a productive meeting? Whatever it is, express gratitude for it. Here are some examples of expressing gratitude throughout the day, making a *conscious* effort to acknowledge and appreciate the good things that come your way.

"I want to express my gratitude to my coworker for their support during the meeting. Their input and collaboration made it a productive, successful session."

"A huge shoutout to my friend who sent me an uplifting, encouraging text message. Their thoughtfulness made me feel loved and supported."

"I'm grateful for the laughter and joy I experienced while watching a funny video online. It reminded me to find moments of lightheartedness and enjoy the simple pleasures in life."

Expressing gratitude throughout the day helps you stay present, appreciate the positive moments, and infuse your day with positivity. By *actively* acknowledging gratitude, you cultivate a mindset of appreciation and invite even more goodness into your life.

Surround yourself with positivity. Choose your company wisely by surrounding yourself with people who radiate positivity, lift your spirits and inspire you to be your best self. Their optimism and support will fuel your gratitude journey.

Try to limit exposure to negativity. Take breaks from social media, especially if you find yourself getting caught up in negative discussions or comparisons. What you consume influences your thoughts and emotions, so be mindful of the content you engage with. Even the physical space around you can reflect positivity and gratitude. Fill your surroundings with uplifting quotes, inspiring artwork, or items that hold special meaning to you.

Practice gratitude with others. Engage in activities or join groups where gratitude and positivity are celebrated. Attend workshops, join gratitude circles, or participate in volunteer projects. Connecting with like-minded individuals can amplify your gratitude journey and provide a supportive community.

Practice self-care Prioritize activities that bring you joy and fulfillment. Engage in hobbies, exercise, spend time in nature, or indulge in self-care practices that recharge your spirit, such as meditation, yoga, painting, drawing, or writing. When you prioritize your own positivity and well-being, you create a strong foundation for gratitude to thrive.

Growth: The Key to Personal Development

Growth is essential for personal development and achieving our full potential. Setting goals and working toward them is one way to grow, but growth goes beyond achieving external accomplishments. It's about continuous learning and improvement. Here are some more practical tips for growth.

Read, read, read. Let the pages become your gateway to new knowledge and endless possibilities. Dedicate at least 15 minutes a day to immerse yourself in books, blogs, and articles on your interests or goals. As you read these very lines, you can already check off today's box on your reading ritual.

Expand your horizons. Actively seek out workshops and seminars that align with your professional or personal passions. These immersive learning experiences offer invaluable opportunities to glean wisdom from experts in the field and connect with others who share your enthusiasm.

Challenge your comfort zone. Wholeheartedly embrace new challenges. By venturing into uncharted territories, you unlock hidden reservoirs of growth, acquiring fresh skills and boosting your confidence along the way. It's through embracing the unknown that you truly discover the depths of your potential.

Have the courage to seek feedback. Constructive criticism, although sometimes hard to hear, holds the key to personal and professional growth. By humbly asking for guidance and insights on how you can improve, you invite valuable perspectives that can propel you forward on your self-development journey. The path to greatness is paved with feedback and a willingness to learn. (Remember to call upon your accountability partner for this one.)

Giving Back: The Gift of Purpose

Giving back to others is an extraordinary act of selflessness that has the power to ignite a sense of purpose and fulfillment within us. It doesn't have to be some grandiose gesture. In fact, it's often the small acts of kindness that ripple out and make a significant impact. Here are some practical ways to help you create a better you by giving back.

Find an organization or cause that resonates with your values and volunteer your time. Whether it's lending a hand at a local shelter by organizing a day of giving, or starting a fundraiser, participating in community events, or supporting educational initiatives, your presence and commitment can create positive change. For example, if you are passionate about supporting the homeless, you can connect with a local nonprofit organization that focuses on providing support and resources to individuals experiencing homelessness. You can volunteer at a homeless shelter or soup kitchen to assist with meal preparation, serving food, or organizing donations.

If you're fortunate enough to have the means, consider making monetary donations to causes close to your heart. When it comes to donating money, it's important to be mindful of where your contribution will be directed. By taking the time to research organizations before making a donation, you can ensure that your generosity is well-placed and can have a significant impact.

Sprinkle kindness like confetti. Practice random acts of kindness in your daily life. Pay for the person behind you in line at a local coffee shop, leave an uplifting note for someone who helped you at the bank, or simply offer a genuine compliment to brighten someone's day. Better yet, let your smile be contagious and share it with everyone you encounter during your daily adventures. Witness how swiftly those smiles come back to you!

Become a mentor. Share your knowledge, skills, and expertise to help others grow and reach their potential. Mentoring is a powerful way to give back. Examples include career mentorship, academic mentorship, entrepreneurial mentorship, personal development mentorship, and youth mentorship. Be the spark that ignites some-one's journey to success.

Incorporating gratitude, growth, and giving back into your daily routine can transform your life in countless ways. By practicing grat-itude, seeking growth opportunities, and giving back to others, you can create a life of purpose and meaning. Giving back is not only about the impact it has on others; it also feeds our own souls. It's not always about achieving external accomplishments or making more money. It's about living a life that is aligned with your values and brings you joy. Start small, be consistent, and watch as your life transforms before your eyes.

H

HABITS

"If I must be a slave to habit, let me be a slave to good habits."—*Og Mandino*

———

I cannot emphasize enough the importance of creating good habits. Habits are those repetitive behaviors you do without much thought and can either nurture or hinder the growth of your passions, which will ultimately determine your success. Thoughts lead to actions. Actions, over time, become habits, and habits lead to long-lasting results.

Let's look at both positive and negative habits.

Positive Habits

- Waking up early and starting your day with intention can lead to increased productivity, better time management, and improved mental health.
- Practicing gratitude and focusing on the positive can lead to a more optimistic outlook, better problem-solving skills, and a greater sense of fulfillment.

- Networking and building relationships can lead to valuable connections, increased opportunities, and a more expansive support system.
- Setting clear goals and creating a plan of action can lead to greater motivation, more focused efforts, and increased levels of success.
- Regular exercise and prioritizing physical health can lead to improved physical and mental well-being, increased energy levels, and improved self-confidence.

Negative Habits

- Procrastinating and putting off important tasks can lead to increased stress and diminished productivity.
- Complaining and dwelling on the negative can lead to a fixed mindset, decreased motivation, and lowered self-esteem.
- Isolating oneself and avoiding social interaction can lead to missed opportunities, decreased support, and increased feelings of loneliness.
- Sedentary lifestyles and neglecting physical health can lead to decreased physical and mental well-being, low energy levels, and increased health risks.

Positive habits can pave the way for building a successful, fulfilling life that aligns with your mission, vision, and values. Cultivating positive habits such as waking up at the same time every day, practicing gratitude, networking, and goal-setting can lead to greater productivity, improved mental health, and increased levels of motivation. On the other hand, negative habits such as procrastination, taking on too much, and a lack of planning can slow your progress and impede your ability to achieve your goals.

It is essential to recognize and break negative habits and replace them with positive ones that will lay the foundation for your success. By doing so, you will find that it becomes easier to take consistent action toward your goals, leading to a sense of accomplishment and fulfillment.

When you develop positive habits, you establish a framework for success that will allow you to excel in every aspect of your life.

At this point, you might be asking yourself, "How long does it take to form a habit?" According to some studies, habits typically take two to three months to form; however, some may take longer or shorter. (Psych Central. (n.d.). Need to Form a New Habit? Here's Your 3-Step Plan. Retrieved from https://psychcentral.com/health/need-to-form-a-new-habit#tips)

Here are a few tips to form some new habits.

Start small. If you want to practice mindfulness, locate a peaceful area, settle in, and concentrate on your breathing. Breathe deeply and slowly, focusing on how it feels to inhale and exhale. Start with a short amount of time, and then progressively extend it. This little habit, if practiced regularly, can improve your general well-being.

Break down your goal into simple steps. Maybe you have a goal to run a 5k. Start by walking, then running at 2–3-minute intervals for the first few weeks, then keep increasing the running time. There are a ton of programs and mobile apps that provide structured training plans and guide your progression.

Find a habit buddy. Having a habit buddy can bring additional motivation, encouragement, and a sense of camaraderie as you work toward your goals together. Find a habit buddy who shares your aspirations and embark on your journey of positive change side by side.

Make time for your habit to develop. Scheduling time for your new habit is essential. Digital reminders and scheduling programs can offer a way for you to ensure there's time in your day to honor your new habit. For example, if your habit involves reading, you can designate 30 minutes before bedtime to unwind and immerse yourself in a good book. This regular practice can help you relax and expand your knowledge.

Reward yourself. Habits are a part of learning, and learning is encouraged by reward. Reward yourself. If your goal is to run a 5K and in the first two weeks you are trotting one mile, reward yourself with new running shorts or a tank top once you've met that goal. This will create positive reinforcement and boost our internal morale. (There is a chapter dedicated to rewarding yourself and others coming up.)

So what about bad habits? How do you break them?

I recently had a conversation with one of my daughters about negative thoughts and anxiety. Back when I studied psychology, I learned aversion-therapy, a form of psychological treatment in which the patient is exposed to a stimulus while simultaneously being subjected to some form of discomfort. Put a rubber band around your wrist, and if stress or a negative thought arises, lightly snap the band. It works because your brain will begin unconsciously avoiding the stimulus (in this case, the negative thought) in order to stop the uncomfortable rubber band from snapping.

The key to breaking bad habits is to identify your triggers, find healthier ways to cope, set goals, and hold yourself accountable. Always seek the advice of a qualified professional, such as a doctor or therapist, regarding any specific habit or behavior you are looking to address.

Here are some common bad habits and ways you can kick them.

Smoking: Identify your motivation for quitting and use it as a source of inspiration.

You might want to seek help from a counselor. They can provide valuable assistance in the process of quitting smoking by offering personalized strategies, addressing underlying factors, providing emotional support, developing coping skills, and offering relapse prevention strategies.

Eating sugar: Reduce your intake gradually, rather than quitting cold turkey.

Find healthy substitutes, such as fruit or honey.

Read food labels to avoid hidden sources of sugar.

Identify your triggers, such as stress or boredom, and find healthier ways to cope.

Procrastination: Break tasks into smaller, manageable steps.

Use a planner or calendar to stay organized and prioritize tasks.

Set goals and hold yourself accountable and share your goals with your accountability partner.

Eliminate distractions, such as social media or television, during work or study time.

Nail biting: Identify your triggers, such as stress or boredom.

Keep your hands busy with a stress ball or fidget spinner.

Wear gloves or put tape on your nails to prevent biting.

Reward yourself for progress, such as with a manicure or new nail polish.

I

"I AM" STATEMENTS

"I am" _____.

_____

The language you use to talk to yourself can either lift you up or tear you down, and the words you use have a profound impact on your thoughts, feelings, and actions. The world can be a difficult and unpleasant place as it is, and you might feel like you are being unfairly judged or deemed unworthy. It's important to avoid falling victim to self-criticism. Instead, concentrate on internalizing your own voice and treating yourself kindly when your inner voice might not be beneficial. You have the power to change that.

"I am" statements are powerful tools for self-affirmation and personal growth. By consciously using positive "I am" statements, you can shift your mindset and edit your thoughts to focus on your strengths, capabilities, and positive qualities. Embracing "I am" statements allows you to challenge self-doubt and negative self-talk, replacing them with empowering, uplifting declarations. By consistently reinforcing positive beliefs about yourself, you cultivate a strong sense of self-confidence, improve your mental health, and foster a more optimistic outlook on life. Incorporating "I am" statements into your daily routine is a simple yet effective way to nurture self-love, enhance self-esteem, and manifest a positive self-image.

Crafting effective I am statements requires thought and intention. Here are some practical tips to help you get started.

Be specific. Instead of using generic statements like "I am successful," try to be more specific about what you want to achieve. For example, "I am a successful business owner" or "I am a successful writer." This helps to create a clear vision of what success looks like for you.

Use the present tense. When creating "I am" statements, it's important to use the present tense. This helps to reinforce the idea that you are already living the life you want, rather than waiting for it to happen in the future. For example, think "I am a writer," vs. "I am thinking of becoming a writer."

Stay positive. Avoid using negative language in your "I am" statements. Instead of saying, "I am not afraid of failure," try saying, "I am confident in my abilities to succeed." Keeping your "I am" statements positive is important because our thoughts and words have a powerful impact on our emotions and actions. When we use negative language (like not, can't, won't, fail, etc.), we reinforce negative thought patterns and beliefs, which can lead to feelings of inadequacy and self-doubt. Treat those like bad words.

On the other hand, when we use positive language in our "I am" statements, we reinforce positive thought patterns and beliefs, which can lead to feelings of self-confidence and empowerment. By focusing on what we can do and what we are capable of, rather than what we can't do or what we fear, we are more likely to take positive action toward our goals.

Now, let's look at some examples of effective "I am" statements.

"I am a confident public speaker who captivates my audience."

"I am a successful entrepreneur making an impact on the world."

"I am a compassionate listener who offers support and under-standing to those around me."

"I am a creative problem-solver who finds solutions to even the most complex challenges."

By using "I am" statements, you create a positive self-image and shift your mindset toward success and achievement.

I want you to practice. Repeat after me:

"I am capable of achieving greatness, and I believe in my abilities to overcome all challenges that may come my way. I am deserving of love, success, and all the blessings life has to offer. I embrace my strengths, and I use them to navigate my journey toward a purposeful, fulfilling life. I am worthy."

Personal Sidenote

Using sticky notes with "I am" statements posted where you'll see them is a great way to reinforce positive affirmations and keep them top of mind. Placing them on your mirror, your laptop (as a screen-saver), or on the back of your phone will remind you of your strengths and keep you motivated.

I have used sticky notes with "I am" statements with great success. I started by writing down a list of affirmations that resonated with me and aligned with my goals and placed them all over my bathroom mirror (bless my husband for not removing them!), so that I would see them every morning when I got ready for the day.

Try it out! The two most powerful words in the English language are "I am." What comes after those two little words can profoundly shape your life.

J
JOY

"Joy does not simply happen to us. We have to choose joy and keep choosing it every day."—Henri J.M. Nouwen

———

What do you think when you hear the word JOY?

Love?

Fun?

Contentment?

A sense of pride or calm?

Happiness?

Finding joy in your daily life is not just about having fun; it's also about cultivating a positive mindset and attitude that can help you overcome challenges and achieve your goals. It's also important for your overall well-being and success. Joy can be found in small moments of pleasure, such as a good cup of coffee, a walk outside in nature, or a conversation with a friend. I believe that happiness and joy are interchangeable, as both emotions bring a sense of positivity and contentment. Recognizing moments of joy can be part of your daily gratitude writing practice as well. Let's dive a little deeper into some reasons why finding joy every day is important.

Joy boosts mood and energy levels. When we experience joy, our brains undergo a fascinating chemical response. Neurotransmitters like dopamine, serotonin, and endorphins are released as a result. These chemicals have a big impact on how our moods are controlled and how emotions of pleasure and well-being are produced. They are our "feel-good" chemicals. They encourage us to continue doing things that make us happy and improve our general sense of well-being.

Joy improves health and well-being. Positive emotions can directly impact our physical health. For example, people who experience positive emotions like joy and happiness can have lower levels of inflammation in their bodies, which can contribute to a range of health problems. People who reported higher levels of positive emotions had better immune system functioning, leading to fewer illnesses and faster recovery times. Research shows that individuals with a more positive emotional style were less likely to develop cold symptoms in response to exposure to the virus. (Cohen, S., Doyle, W. J., Turner, R. B., Alper, C. M., and Skoner, D. P. (2003). Emotional style and susceptibility to the common cold. *Psychosomatic Medicine,* 65(4), 652-657.)

Joy enhances relationships. When we're happy and joyful, we're more likely to radiate positive energy and connect with others on a deeper level, fostering more meaningful relationships. Our state of happiness makes us approachable, open, and receptive, allowing for authentic, fulfilling connections. People are naturally drawn to those who exude joy and happiness because it creates an inviting, uplifting environment.

When we share our happiness with others, it has a ripple effect. Our positive outlook can inspire and uplift those around us, encouraging them to find joy in their own lives. The contagious nature of happiness can create a chain reaction, influencing our immediate circle and also extending to our communities and beyond.

Now that you know what joy can do, here are some tips on how you can cultivate it in your daily life.

Practice gratitude. (Chapter G covers this in great lengths.) Make it a habit to list things you're grateful for every day. This can help you focus on the positive aspects of your life and cultivate a sense of joy and appreciation.

Engage in activities that bring you joy. Whether it's listening to music, practicing yoga, or painting, make time for activities that bring you pleasure and fulfillment.

Surround yourself with positive people. Spend time with people who uplift and inspire you. Seek out friends and mentors who share your values and goals.

Journal. Journaling is an excellent tool for cultivating joy and personal growth. It can help you reflect on your emotions, track your progress, and set goals for the future. Here are two ways to use journaling to cultivate joy.

- The Joy Journal: Record moments of joy and pleasure that you experience throughout the day, like seeing a beautiful bird, listening to music or a favorite podcast, reading a good book, watching a favorite movie, cooking a delicious meal, or trying out a new recipe.
- The Self-Reflection Journal: Reflect on your emotions, thoughts, and behaviors to gain insight and perspective, like: What are some of the relationships in my life that are most important to me, and how can I nurture and strengthen them? What are my top values in life, and how am I living up to them? What is one thing I can do today to take care of myself?

Finding joy every day is essential for our overall well-being and success. Using journaling as a tool for self-reflection and personal growth, we can increase our happiness, strengthen our relationships, and achieve our goals. Take some time each day to focus on joy and watch it transform your life.

Personal Sidenote

People often ask me these questions:

"What can't you do, Elaine?"

"You're always doing something or trying something new."

"Don't you ever stop?"

"When do you sleep?" (My favorite. Insert eye roll.)

"What motivates you to keep pushing yourself and trying new things?"

I believe that life is full of opportunities, and I strive to make the most of them. I'm always eager to seek out new experiences and challenges that help me learn and grow as a person. I have a sense of adventure and a desire to broaden my horizons, which motivates me to try new hobbies, enroll in classes, or pursue new objectives. Of course, I also prioritize rest, relaxation, and self-care because they are essential for maintaining balance and well-being.

For me, the key to a happy, fulfilling life is engaging in activities that bring me unbridled *joy*. Crocheting is one of my favorite pastimes because it's relaxing and also a chance for me to reflect on my mom, who taught me so much about crafting. I also love trying new recipes, not just for my own enjoyment but also to share them with our café customers and nourish their bodies and souls. I love shooting headshots because who wouldn't love a job that requires people to smile at you all the time? I could do that every day!

However, joy doesn't just come from hobbies and work. I find happiness in other ways, too. Volunteering, going on walks alone while listening to inspiring podcasts, making videos of DIY projects, using only dollar store items to help others create on a budget, sitting with hospice patients to learn about their life journey, bringing back carts at the grocery store, and simply smiling at strangers or complimenting other women on their amazing smiles—these are just a few of the ways I find joy in my everyday life.

When we focus on doing things that bring us joy, we feel happier and also more fulfilled. And when we're fulfilled, we can make a positive impact on those around us, too. I hope to inspire others to find their own sources of joy and fulfillment and to help them spread that joy wherever they go.

Additionally, writing this book has been an incredibly fulfilling experience for me. Not only have I been able to reflect on my own journey and share my insights with you, but I also know that this book has the potential to reach thousands of people and, in turn, spread joy and inspiration. Knowing that my words could have a positive impact on someone else's life brings me immense joy and motivation to keep sharing my message with the world.

I choose joy.

K

KEEP CALM (AND SAY NO)

"Opportunity seldom rises with blood pressure." —*Jarod Kintz*

Do you ever feel like you're running a marathon every day, trying to keep up with the demands of work, family, and life? Do you struggle finding time to write in your gratitude journal or even meditate for five minutes? You're not alone. We all experience stress and feelings of being overwhelmed at times, and it's important to develop strategies for managing these feelings.

In this chapter, we'll explore practical ways to keep calm and centered, even in the midst of chaos. You'll learn how to prioritize self-care, practice mindfulness, set boundaries, and seek support when needed. By developing these skills, you can reduce stress, find greater balance, and live a more fulfilling life.

Prioritize self-care. This means taking care of your physical, mental, and emotional well-being. It's easy to neglect self-care when you're busy, but it's essential for managing stress and maintaining your overall health. You can start by getting enough sleep, eating a healthy diet, or starting an exercise regimen. Make time for activities that you enjoy, such as reading, listening to music, or spending time with loved ones.

Practice mindfulness. Mindfulness is the practice of being present in the moment without judgment. It can help you stay calm and centered, even when you're feeling stressed or anxious. You can practice mindfulness in many ways, such as through meditation, deep breathing, or simply taking a few moments to focus on your senses and surroundings. By cultivating mindfulness, you can develop a greater sense of awareness and control over your thoughts and emotions.

Setting Boundaries (Also Known as "The Power of No")

"Almost everything will work if you unplug it for a few minutes, including you."—Anne Lamott

One of the most important things you can do to manage stress is to learn to say no. This one is my favorite, and one of the most powerful tools in your toolbox. Saying no helps you become more aware of your mission, vision, and values. It's easy to fall into the trap of trying to do it all, but the reality is that we can't. It's okay to say no to requests that don't align with your priorities or plan. It can be tempting to say yes to every request that comes our way, whether it's from our boss, family, or friends. However, when we say yes to everything, we can quickly become overcommitted, resentful, angry, and overwhelmed. Saying no allows us to prioritize our own needs and boundaries and communicate our limitations to others.

Times where it's ok to say, no.

Social events: It's okay to decline invitations to social events if you're feeling overwhelmed or if the event doesn't align with your interests or values.

Additional work projects: If your workload is already full or you're feeling stretched thin, it's okay to say no to taking on *additional* work projects (if you have a say in the matter).

Volunteer opportunities: While it's important to give back to your community, it's okay to decline volunteer opportunities that don't fit with your schedule or interests.

Requests for help: While it's good to help others when we can, it's okay to say no to requests for help if it's not feasible or if it would be too much of a burden on you.

Let's see it in action.

Person A: I wanted to invite you to this party next weekend. It's going to be a huge gathering with lots of people. Are you interested in coming?

Person B: Thank you so much for the invitation! I appreciate it, but I'm looking forward to a relaxing weekend at home. I'll have to pass on this one, but I hope you have a great time at the party.

———

Person A: I heard you're good at graphic design. We have this additional project that needs some design work, and we were wondering if you could take it on?

Person B: Thanks for thinking of me and recognizing my skills! I'm currently working on a few projects with tight deadlines, and I want to ensure I can give my best to those. I'll have to say no to this additional project, but I appreciate the opportunity.

———

It's important to be honest with yourself and with others about your limitations and boundaries. By saying no when you need to, you can prioritize your own well-being and find greater balance and fulfillment in your life.

"When you say 'yes' to others make sure you are not saying 'no' to yourself."—
Paulo Coelho

Seek Support

If you're struggling with stress or other challenges, it's important to reach out for help. Talking to a trusted friend or family member can offer emotional support, understanding, and a listening ear. Sometimes, simply expressing your feelings and concerns out loud can bring a sense of relief and clarity.

However, if you find that your stress or challenges persist or worsen, it might be beneficial to seek guidance from a mental health professional. These trained professionals can provide specialized support, offer coping strategies, and help you develop effective ways to manage stress and overcome obstacles. They can also diagnose and treat any underlying mental health conditions that may be contributing to your challenges.

Remember, seeking support is a sign of strength, not weakness. It takes courage to acknowledge when you need assistance to take proactive steps to improve your well-being. Whether through counseling, support groups, or helplines, resources are available to provide the support you need.

Managing stress, finding balance, and maintaining your focus on what's truly important are essential for living a healthy and productive life. As the saying goes, "You can't pour from an empty cup." When we neglect our own needs and well-being, it's difficult to show up as our best selves in other areas of our lives So take a deep breath, focus on what's truly important, and remember to take care of yourself along the way. With a little bit of effort and intention, you can keep calm and manage stress like a pro.

———

Personal Sidenote

There are many ways I unwind daily. Whether I do a craft, listen to a podcast (I'm a huge true crime junkie), do my nails, read, crochet, or clean the house (yes, it's calming for me, because when it's not clean, I'm stressed!). I always manage to find a way to unwind, and one of my favorite ways to do this is to *float*.

Float?

Yes! Float! In a tub of water. In complete darkness. I hear nothing but my eyes blinking and my heart beating.

A float tank, also known as a sensory deprivation tank, is a small, enclosed tank or tub filled with a foot or more of water and a high concentration of Epsom salt. The water is heated to skin temperature, creating a sense of weightlessness, to allow the body to float effortlessly. (Think of the Dead Sea.)

The lack of sensory input can be incredibly relaxing and restorative for the mind and body, allowing for deep relaxation and a sense of calm. During my first float, I only lasted about 20 minutes (the session is 70 minutes!). By the third time, I had made it all the way, and it felt like I had only been in it for about 10 minutes.

Some of the benefits of using a float tank to unwind include:

- Reducing stress and anxiety: The sensory deprivation and relaxation of a float tank can help reduce levels of stress hormones like cortisol, leading to feelings of calm and relaxation.
- Relieving chronic pain: The high concentration of Epsom salt in the water can help relieve sore muscles and joints and promote healing.
- Improving sleep: Deep relaxation and a reduction in stress can help improve sleep quality and reduce insomnia.
- Enhancing creativity and focus: Sensory deprivation can help promote a state of hyper-awareness, allowing for enhanced creativity, problem-solving, and focus. This is my favorite part! When I come out, I feel like I have a natural high, which, for me, lasts for days! (Some of my best ideas and creations come after a float!)

Overall, the use of a float tank can be a powerful tool for shutting down and promoting relaxation and inner peace. You should ask your healthcare provider before using a float tank, especially if you have any medical conditions or concerns.

L

LET GO AND LET LOVE

"If you're searching for that one person who will change your life…take a look in the mirror."—*Unknown*

The Power of Self-Love and Positive Emotions

Letting go of unfavorable feelings, constricting ideas, and painful past experiences is a necessary step on the path to living a fulfilling life. Forgiving yourself and others, letting go of the emotions that no longer serve you, and developing inner peace are all part of the process of letting go. This is where the power of love comes in, both for you and those around you. Self-love empowers us to approach each day with love from the inside. When we cultivate love for ourselves, we radiate positivity and kindness toward others. Our interactions become infused with empathy, understanding, and compassion, creating a ripple effect that touches the lives of those around us. In this chapter, we'll explore how to *let go and let love* and why it's crucial to greet each day with love in our hearts. By letting go of past hurts, we free ourselves from the shackles of negativity and create space for healing, personal development, and more fulfilling relationships.

Letting Go of Negative Emotions

We all experience negative emotions at some point in our lives. However, it's important to learn how to release them. Holding on to negative emotions like anger, resentment, and guilt only hurts us and prevents us from moving forward. When we learn to let go of negative emotions, we can experience a sense of peace and freedom that allows us to live more fully.

One way to let go of negative emotions is through forgiveness, a powerful tool that enables us to release anger and hurt that we might be carrying.

While forgiveness can be a transformative process in many situations, it is equally important to acknowledge that it does not mean condoning or forgetting what has transpired. Forgiveness does not negate the significance of the hurt or the need for accountability. Instead, it involves a conscious decision to let go of the negative emotions tied to the experience and to free ourselves from the burden of carrying resentment. Forgiveness is a personal process that primarily benefits the person who forgives. It does not release an offender from their accountability or justify their behavior.

Author's note: In instances where forgiveness might not be suitable, it is crucial to seek support from trusted individuals, such as therapists, counselors, or support groups, who can provide guidance and assistance in navigating complex emotions and healing processes. By recognizing and honoring our boundaries, we can prioritize our well-being while still actively working toward personal growth and emotional healing.

Remember, the journey toward letting go and embracing *self-love* involves honoring our own experiences and finding the most appropriate paths to healing and growth. It is through understanding our own needs and seeking support when necessary that we can navigate the complexities of forgiveness and emotional release, ultimately fostering a healthier, more fulfilling life.

Here are three tips for practicing forgiveness and self-love.

Use positive I am affirmations. Repeat positive affirmations to yourself, such as I am choosing to forgive or I am letting go of the past. This can help shift your mindset toward forgiveness and release negative emotions.

Seek support. Reach out to a trusted friend, family member, or therapist to talk about your feelings and get support. Sometimes talking about the situation can help you gain perspective and let go of negative emotions.

Focus on the present. Instead of ruminating about the past, concentrate on the present moment and the positive things in your life. By shifting your focus to the present, you can let go of negative emotions and move forward toward a more positive future.

Cultivating Positive Emotions

Cultivating positive emotions like love, joy, and gratitude can have a profound impact on our lives. When we focus on positive emotions, we attract more positive experiences and people into our lives. By making a conscious effort to focus on positive emotions and practicing gratitude regularly, we can train our minds to seek out and appreciate the good in our lives.

Another way to cultivate positive emotions is through *random acts of kindness*. When we do something for someone else, it not only makes them feel good, but it also makes us feel good. Acts of kindness can be as simple as holding the door open for someone or sending a thoughtful message to a friend.

Here are ten acts of love and kindness you can do to show others love and positivity:

1. Send a thoughtful message or card to a friend or loved one to brighten their day.
2. Cook a meal or bake a treat for a neighbor or friend.
3. Volunteer at a local charity or organization.

4. Compliment someone and acknowledge their strengths and talents.
5. Offer to help someone with a task or project they're struggling with.
6. Provide support by "actively" listening to someone who might not be looking for advice but rather someone to just sit with them in their time of need.
7. Do something unexpected and spontaneous for someone you care about.
8. Offer a smile or a kind word to a stranger you encounter in your day.
9. Share your own experiences and wisdom to help someone going through a difficult time.
10. Encourage someone to pursue their dreams and goals and offer support along the way.

Greeting Each Day with Love

The power of love starts with loving ourselves first. When we love ourselves, we're able to show up fully in our relationships with others. It's important to take time each day to nurture ourselves, whether that's through exercise, meditation, or simply taking a few minutes to relax and unwind.

Once we've nurtured ourselves, we can extend love to others. This includes our family, friends, coworkers, and even strangers. When we greet each day with love in our hearts, we're able to see the good in others and approach situations with a positive mindset.

The Power of "I Love You"

"I love you" is one of the most powerful sentences in the English language. When we say these words to ourselves, we're affirming our self-worth and acknowledging that we're deserving of love. When we say these words to others, we're showing them that they're important to us and that we care about them.

Want to experiment? Try this simple task for the next week. Every time you interact with someone, whether it's a loved one, a friend, or even a stranger, look them in the eye and say I love you *to yourself*, but emit it toward them.

Notice how this simple act of love and kindness impacts your inter-actions with others. You might notice that people respond more positively to you, that you feel more connected to those around you, or that you simply feel better about yourself. By expressing love to those around you, you're cultivating positivity and spreading kind-ness in the world.

Take the challenge and see how it feels to greet each day with love in your heart and express it to those around you. Letting go of nega-tive emotions and embracing love and positivity is crucial for living a fulfilling life. Learning to love ourselves first is key to this process. By greeting each day with love in our hearts, we're able to approach life with a positive mindset and attract more positive experiences and people into our lives. So take time each day to nurture yourself, practice gratitude, and extend love to others. And always remember the power of I love you—to yourself and to others. You might be surprised at how much it can transform your life and the lives of those around you.

Personal Sidenote

During one of my workshops a few years ago, I was discussing the importance of love and self-love. Suddenly, I had an idea that would help drive home the message in a fun, engaging way. I stopped talking and hit play on my computer. The infectious beat of "I Love Me" by Meghan Trainor filled the room, and I asked everyone to stand up and join me. She sings about the importance of loving yourself, even if those around you don't.

We danced and sang along to the lyrics. (Check it out on YouTube.)

The energy in the room shifted. It was a powerful moment as we all connected with the message of self-love and felt the positive impact it can have on our lives.

This experience was a reminder of the power of music and movement to inspire and connect us. It also showed how simple activities, like dancing and singing, can help us internalize an important message and make it a part of our lives.

The next time you need a boost of love and positivity, put on your favorite song and dance like no one's watching. It might feel silly at first, but who cares? Try it right now and see how it feels. I promise you'll laugh!

M

MISSION STATEMENT

"Go forward in life with a twinkle in your eye and a smile on your face, but with great purpose in heart."—*Gordon B. Hinckley*

———

A personal mission statement is the foundation upon which you can build a fulfilling, purpose-driven life. In this chapter, we'll explore why a personal mission statement is central to defining your vision and values, and how it can help you unlock your gifts and live with purpose. I'll also guide you through creating your own.

Let's talk about some of the benefits of having a personal mission statement.

It provides clarity and focus. By identifying what is truly important to you, you can prioritize your time and energy on what matters most, which keeps you focused on your goals.

It aids in decision-making. When you have a clear sense of your values and objectives, it becomes easier to evaluate choices and make decisions that align with your long-term goals.

It's motivating. It acts as a source of inspiration, encouraging you to push through challenges and stay committed to your goals.

It fosters accountability and responsibility. It serves as a reminder of the commitments you've made to yourself and others.

Creating a personal mission statement requires self-reflection and introspection. By gaining a better understanding of your strengths, weaknesses, and aspirations, you can work toward becoming the best version of yourself.

Now that you understand the benefits of the personal mission statement, let's create one.

Step One

Jot down everything related to yourself and your business, including descriptions of your work, your identity, your target audience, amusing anecdotes, interesting facts, and your passions. Here are some prompts to help you.

- Your hobbies and interests
- Your personal values and beliefs
- Your strengths and weaknesses
- What you enjoy doing in your free time
- Your proudest accomplishments
- People you like to work with
- Your life goals and aspirations
- Your favorite books, movies, or TV shows
- Your role models and inspirations
- Any challenges or obstacles you've overcome
- Your favorite quotes or mantras

Let your thoughts flow freely. Don't worry about being perfect or concise; you can always edit and refine it later. The goal is to get everything out of your head and onto paper. Once you have your list, you can start to narrow it down by identifying the elements that resonate with you the most.

Step Two

Now it's time to identify the "who" elements—a crucial step in creating a personal mission statement. This is where you get to focus on who you want to impact and how you want to make a difference. Using a red pen, circle all the people or groups that you feel drawn to helping, serving, or empowering. This can include individuals, communities, organizations, or even the world at large. The key is to identify the people or groups that resonate with you the most.

For example, you might circle "women" if you feel passionate about advocating for gender equality and empowering women to achieve their full potential. Or, you might circle "nonprofits" if you feel drawn to supporting organizations that are working toward a specific cause, such as environmental conservation or social justice.

Other examples of "who" elements you might circle could be men, children, entrepreneurs, network marketers, boutique owners, small businesses, lawyers, nurses, writers, stay-at-home moms, and many more. The goal is to identify the people or groups that align with your values and purpose and that you feel inspired to serve.

Step Three

After identifying your "who" elements, it's time to think about how you can impact or serve them. This is where the "how" elements come into play. The "how" elements are the actions you take to make a difference for the people or groups you've identified.

To begin identifying your "how" elements, highlight the actions you take to make a difference. These can include—but are not limited to:

- Creating
- Teaching
- Purchasing
- Preparing
- Mending

- Telling stories
- Writing
- Inspiring
- Speaking
- Connecting
- Giving

For example, if you circled "women" as one of your "who" elements, you might highlight actions like teaching, mentoring, or advocating for your "how." If you circled "non-profits" as one of your "who" elements, you might highlight actions like donating, volunteering, or fundraising for non-profit organizations for your "how."

The "how" elements are important because they help you identify the specific actions you can take to make a difference for the people or groups you wish to serve. By highlighting these actions, you can begin to see how you can use your unique talents, skills, and resources to create an impact. The more creative and specific you can be with your "how" elements, the more powerful your personal mission statement will be.

Step Four

The fourth step in creating your personal mission statement is to underline the outcomes of your efforts. This step is about identifying the difference you want to make on the people or groups you've identified, and how you hope they'll feel as a result of your work and contributions.

Think about the difference you want to make in the world. What changes do you want to affect? What ideas do you want to share? What do you hope to empower others to do?

Once you have identified the difference you want to make, think about how you hope people will feel because of your work. Do you want them to feel inspired, empowered, or uplifted? Do you want to create a sense of community, connection, or belonging? Do you want to bring joy, beauty, or creativity into their lives? Maybe all of the above?

Here are some examples of outcomes and/or desired feelings you might underline when creating your personal mission statement:

Outcomes: inspiring positive change, promoting sustainability, fostering inclusivity, advancing social justice, improving health and well-being, providing educational opportunities, supporting artistic expression, and creating economic opportunities.

Desired feelings: empowerment, joy, hope, connectedness, inspiration, fulfillment, creativity, gratitude, and resilience.

For instance, if you want to inspire positive change and promote sustainability, you might underline "improving environmental health" as an outcome, and "creating a sense of responsibility and stewardship" as a desired feeling. If you want to support artistic expression, you might underline "fostering creativity and self-expression" as an outcome, and "creating a sense of wonder and appreciation for the arts" as a desired feeling.

Remember, your outcomes and desired feelings should reflect your unique values, strengths, and aspirations. They should inspire and motivate you to take action toward your goals.

Now it's time to bring it all together. Integrate your who's, how's, and the impact you hope to make. Your mission statement should be concise and captured in a single sentence or two. Experiment with various combinations, and when you read it aloud, it should take no more than 20 to 30 seconds to recite.

For example, a personal mission statement for a writer might look like this.

"My mission is to inspire and empower young artists through storytelling that sparks transformative change, encourages personal growth, and fosters authentic connections."

A personal mission statement for a small business owner might look like this:

"My mission is to create a welcoming, inclusive space that supports and empowers all entrepreneurs, offering resources and guidance to help them thrive and succeed."

No matter what your personal mission statement looks like, it should reflect your unique talents, passions, and aspirations and inspire you to take action toward your goals.

Once you have created your personal mission statement, refer to it regularly and use it as a guiding principle when making decisions and setting goals. By doing so, you'll stay true to yourself and live a more fulfilling, intentional life.

———

Personal Sidenote

When I wrote my own personal mission statement five years ago, everything changed for me. Although I wish I had kept the original yellow legal pad with all my notes on it, the process of creating my own mission statement was transformative. I wrote for two or three days, jotting down fragments, slogans, short stories, jokes, thoughts, memories, and ideas. My goal was to create a statement that reflected my purpose, personality, and background—not just that of my business or career, but my true essence and reason for being.

Originally, I crafted the statement "to empower women to use their gifts and talents to rise and soar." I used this for about two to three years; however, as I evolved and grew, I realized I needed more "outcomes." Thus, my current personal mission statement as of this writing is:

"To empower women to use their gifts and talents to rise and soar by helping them level up their craft and build an abundant life and business."

My mission statement identifies my target audience as "women." Even though I work with everyone, my work is more female-focused.

The "how" element of my statement is to empower, inspire, and teach.

The desired "impact" (outcome and feelings) I strive for include helping others live a more purposeful and abundant life using their own talents and crafts.

Scan this QR code to download the easy-to-follow mission statement guide.

N

NEW

How do you typically respond to change?

Are you excited by it, or do you tend to resist it?

When's the last time you tried something new?

Embracing new opportunities and experiences is essential to growth and success. Consistently broadening our horizons and pushing ourselves outside of our comfort zones is the key to leading a happy, meaningful life. We'll discuss the importance of accepting new possibilities in this chapter, along with useful tips for overcoming fear, developing resilience, and moving closer to a life of abundance.

Our world is continuously changing, and people who are open to new possibilities and eager to take advantage of new chances will thrive. Trying something new, whether it's a career, relationship, or hobby, can be both exhilarating and terrifying at the same time. If we allow fear to hold us back, we run the risk of missing out on amazing chances for development and personal growth.

I mentioned earlier that embracing something new can be terrifying. Our fears of the future, failure, and rejection can all prevent us from pursuing new opportunities. It's crucial to keep in mind that fear is a normal human emotion that we all experience. The trick is to recognize our fear and go forward despite it, rather than letting it rule us. Here are some practical strategies.

Start small. If the idea of trying anything new feels intimidating, start with something small. Take an alternative route to work, visit a new restaurant, or read a book of a different genre. Making these small changes can boost your confidence and make the thought of attempting something more difficult seem less intimidating.

Focus on the positive. When we focus on the negative, we can easily talk ourselves out of just about anything. Instead, focus on the potential benefits and what you might gain from the experience. For example, instead of worrying about the potential awkwardness of attending a networking event, focus on the opportunity to meet new people and expand your professional network. If you're nervous about speaking up in a meeting, focus on the positive impact that your knowledge and expertise could bring to the project. When considering a career change, focus on the potential for personal and professional growth rather than the uncertainty of the job market.

Take calculated risks. Taking risks is an essential part of embracing the new, but it's important to be strategic about it. Consider the potential risks and rewards before deciding. If the potential rewards outweigh the risks, then it might be worth taking the leap. If you're considering starting your own business, research the market and create a solid business plan before quitting your day job. If you're thinking of moving to a new city for a job opportunity, weigh the potential benefits against the potential challenges of starting fresh in a new place.

Build a support system. Having a support system can make trying something new feel less scary. Remember those accountability partners and collaborators we talked about in Chapters A and C? Talk to friends or family members who have tried something similar or seek out a mentor who can offer guidance and support. If you're considering going back to school, talk to someone who has recently completed a similar program to get their insights and advice. If you're considering making a big life change (like starting a new career), seek out a mentor or coach who can offer guidance and support.

Success Story: From Health and Wellness Enthusiast to Network Marketing Influencer

Meet Jake, a young professional with a passion for health and wellness. Jake had always found network marketing intriguing, but he had some apprehensions about it because of its bad reputation as it related to pyramid schemes. However, after attending a personal development seminar about high-quality health products—and trying some samples—he decided to give it a chance and signed up as a rep.

Initially, Jake was unsure about how to approach the business and build a network. Instead of letting fear hold him back, he immersed himself in learning and applied the strategies outlined in the seminar. He started by reaching out to friends and family, sharing his personal journey with the company's products and the positive impact they had on his well-being. He focused on building genuine relationships and providing value through education and support.

As Jake expanded his network, he discovered the power of leveraging social media to connect with like-minded individuals interested in health and wellness. He created engaging content and shared his experiences, tips, and success stories. Through consistent effort, he attracted a growing audience and began nurturing relationships with potential customers and business partners alike.

Jake's dedication and authenticity paid off. He experienced personal health transformations and also built a thriving network marketing business. His enthusiasm and belief in the products were contagious, attracting a team of motivated individuals who shared his vision.

As his network grew, Jake embraced his role as a mentor and leader, providing guidance and training to his team members. He understood the importance of supporting and empowering others on their own journeys to success.

Through network marketing, Jake achieved financial freedom and also discovered a deep sense of fulfillment in helping others improve their health and well-being. He became an influential figure in the industry and earned trips and bonuses while inspiring others to embrace network marketing as a viable path to personal and professional growth.

Jake's story shows the power of embracing new opportunities, even if they come with preconceived notions or doubts. By overcoming his reservations and dedicating himself to building a network marketing business, Jake transformed his life and the lives of people around him.

———

Personal Sidenote

The desire to try something new has always been a driving force in my life. It's what led me to where I am today—and to writing this book.

My mother's passing influenced my desire to live life to the fullest, and I honor her memory by embracing new experiences. I often think of the things she never got to do, like go to Italy, take baking classes, and start a craft business.

So trying new things is a passion of mine, whether it's taking an Italian class, trying a new crochet pattern, or starting an organic garden. Very few things make me nervous anymore because I know there are resources out there to help me figure it out. Plus, I have an incredible support system of friends, family, and collaborators who hold me accountable and inspire me to keep pushing forward. If there's something I want to do, I figure out how to do it. I recently renovated my bathroom and turned to YouTube for guidance. Move over Bob Vila! I ripped the entire thing out and reinstalled a shower, toilet, vanity, and flooring.

I try to squash fear as much as I can and empower people around me to do the same. I never want to stop learning or trying new things.

In short, embracing the new has always been a fundamental part of who I am. It's led me to incredible opportunities and amazing people, and I'm excited to share my insights and strategies with others.

O
―――――

ORGANIZE YOUR LIFE

"A good system shortens the road to the goal."—*Orison Swett Marden*

―――――

Do you find yourself constantly juggling tasks and not getting any done?

Do you ever feel like your to-do list is never-ending, and instead of starting, you freeze?

How many projects have you started, but left dormant and still need to finished?

The good news is that there are steps you can take to simplify your routines and lessen this stress. Daily life demands can easily become exhausting. In this chapter, I'll share my favorite tips and tricks for streamlining tasks and minimizing distractions, so you can focus on what's important and achieve more, with less effort. Get ready to simplify your life and discover the benefits of a less-stress lifestyle!

Where do you start?

One of the first steps to simplifying your life is to identify some areas that need improvement. I'll cover a few here, but I'm sure there are a ton more.

- Daily routines
- Schedules
- Social media distractions
- Misalignment

Daily Routines

Daily routines can provide structure and stability in our lives, which help us feel more in control, more fulfilled, and less stressed. By establishing a routine that works for you, you can create a framework for your day that allows you to accomplish your goals and enjoy your free time, all while increasing productivity.

Take a look at your daily routines and identify the ones that take up the most time or cause the most stress. Do you spend a lot of time getting ready in the morning and panicking if you are running late? If so, consider streamlining your routine by picking out your outfit the night before or preparing your breakfast in advance. Pack your bag and lunch the night before, too. This will help you start your day off on the right foot and reduce the stress of rushing in the morning. The same thing goes for your nighttime routine. If you find it difficult to wind down and relax at night, create a bedtime routine that will help you relax and prepare for sleep. This might include reading a book, taking a warm bath, or practicing meditation or yoga.

For me, I hate grocery shopping, and in the words of Sweet Brown from 2012, "Ain't nobody got time for that!" Nowadays, there are apps to help me. When I get stressed about making dinner and the refrigerator is empty, I go on my Giant Food Stores app, order what I need for the next few days, and pick it up when I'm out and about later in the day. It literally saves me about an hour or more. And no, I don't miss walking around the aisles picking out my own bananas; they do a perfectly good job picking out my produce. That little convenience saves me from an additional 20 gray hairs, and it decreases my anxiety. So, win-win!

Another quick thing I do at the end of a workday or on my way home is get gas. I don't know about you, but I absolutely abhor getting in my car in the morning with an empty tank of gas. I'm going places, and I don't have time to run on empty—literally.

Schedules

Now, I know there are a gazillion apps and programs out there to help you keep track of your time and maintain a tight schedule, but I'll let you in on my method.

My old-fashioned 12-month datebook only has 24 pages. Each month is a spread. So twelve spreads are right in front of me. I am allotted a 2x2 square daily to write in my appointments, notes, events, birthdays, and anniversary reminders. That's it. I'm a very visual person, so seeing all my tasks, reminders, appointments, and doodles all in front of me in my own handwriting is key (and calming). This works for me. I sometimes use my phone calendar for backup when I'm on the go; however, this system has been working for me for the past 20 years. I sometimes pick up an old date book, and it's like a trip down memory lane whenever I flip through it. Call me old school, but my trusty date book is here to stay.

I know. I know. I can use Google Calendar or some other app. But what if my phone and computer crash all on the same day? Where am I going? Crazy. That's where I'm going.

However, what if I misplace my datebook? Well, then I'm screwed.

The bottom line and most important thing is to find a system that works for you and stick with it.

I am a block scheduling type of gal. I divide my day into specific time blocks, assigning tasks to each block. This technique helps me stay focused and avoid distractions, as well as ensure that I have enough time to complete all my tasks. For example, I block off two hours in the morning to work on my photography business. I read emails, edit photos, do marketing, and prepare for any upcoming shoots. The next block of time will be spent on Zekraft, our café and catering businesses. I help take care of the social media, graphics, visiting the cafés, training new staff, and scheduling for all our cafés. For that, I give myself a block of two to three hours. The other parts of my day vary. I might block off three hours to write (like I'm doing right now), an hour to go for a walk, exercise, visit the doctor, go to lunch with a friend, or go to a networking event.

The fun part of block scheduling for me is that I reward myself all the time. If I really enjoy writing (which I do), and it's the third block of the day, well, I am not allowed to write until my other blocks are done. I hold myself accountable! It makes me maintain my responsibilities with my husband to hold up my end of the bargain to do my Zekraft duties. I don't procrastinate. I don't waste time. My time is extremely valuable, so I spend it wisely on the things that align with my mission, vision, and values.

Finding a system that works for you is crucial when it comes to managing your schedule and maximizing your productivity. Whether it's an old-fashioned datebook or block scheduling, the key is to find a method that suits your needs and lifestyle. By sticking to a schedule and holding yourself accountable, you can stay on track and accomplish your goals efficiently.

Social Media Distractions

Another practical tip for simplifying your life is to minimize distractions. Distractions can take many forms, such as notifications on your phone or computer, background noise, or clutter in your workspace. To minimize social media distractions, consider turning off notifications during work hours. If you could see me now, I'm writing in my dining room, sitting at the table. My phone is on vibrate (not silent; because I'm a mother, I can't turn it off all the way with three daughters in different parts of the country all the time). I turned off all notifications for my apps because when I need to check in, I will open the app to do so. There's no "Facebook event reminder" emergency in my eyes, and I can live without seeing Tammy with a new puppy for a few hours longer, as well.

Or, better yet, how about a social media detox? A social media detox is a great way to step back and prioritize the things that truly matter in life. By taking a break from the constant noise and distraction of social media, we can gain a fresh perspective and refocus our energy on activities that bring us joy and fulfillment.

If you're feeling overwhelmed by the idea of a full-blown social media detox. Don't worry. You can start small. Begin by taking a break from one or two platforms that you feel are consuming too much of your time and energy. Set a realistic timeframe, whether it's a day, a week, or even longer, and commit to sticking with it.

During your break, use your newfound free time to engage in activities that make you happy, whether it's spending time with loved ones, exploring new hobbies, or finally tackling that project that's been on your to-do list for ages. Maybe it's time to start writing that book you've been dreaming of. Whatever it is, you'll find that you have so much more time and energy to devote to the things that truly matter.

Misalignment

One way to simplify your life while working on your mission, vision, and values is to ensure that your work aligns with your core values. When your work reflects your values, you'll experience a greater sense of purpose and fulfillment. Here's how you can do it.

Identify your core values. Take the time to reflect on your core values and define what is truly important to you. For example, if one of your core values is environmental sustainability, you might prioritize work that promotes eco-friendly practices or contributes to renewable energy solutions.

Evaluate your current work. Assess how well your current work aligns with your core values. Identify aspects that resonate with your values and those that don't. For instance, if you value work-life balance, but find yourself constantly working overtime, it might be a sign that your current work is not in line with your values.

Make adjustments. Consider making adjustments to bring your work into alignment with your core values. This could involve exploring new job opportunities that are more closely aligned with your values. For example, if your core value is social justice, you might consider transitioning to a nonprofit organization or advocacy role.

Set boundaries. Simplify your life by setting boundaries around your work. Determine how much time and energy you're willing to dedicate to work while ensuring you have enough space for other important aspects of your life. For example, you could establish specific work hours and avoid checking emails or taking work-related calls outside of those hours. Remember, it's ok to say no to activities that don't align with what you are building right now.

Regularly review and reflect. Regularly review your progress and reflect on whether your work is still aligned with your mission, vision, and values. This allows you to make necessary adjustments and ensures that you stay on track. Consider scheduling regular self-reflection sessions or seeking feedback from your trusted account-ability partners, mentors, or colleagues.

Organizing your life is about identifying the areas of your life that need improvement and taking practical steps to minimize distractions and maximize productivity. By streamlining your daily routines, scheduling your time effectively, minimizing social media distractions, and being in alignment with your values, you can create a framework for your day that allows you to accomplish your goals and enjoy your free time with less stress and anxiety.

Remember, finding a system that works for you is crucial when it comes to managing your schedule and maximizing your productivity. Don't be afraid to try different methods until you find the one that suits your needs and lifestyle. Organizing and simplifying your life can be challenging, but the benefits of a less-stress lifestyle are worth the effort.

P

POWER OF THE PIVOT

"A key factor in success is knowing when to pivot, to rethink your plan, while still maintaining the mission."—Camille Sweeney and Josh Gossfield

---

Let's talk about the power of the pivot and how it can help you succeed in today's rapidly changing world. Pivoting can be exciting and not nearly as daunting or irritating as hearing the character Ross Geller shout, "Pivot!" repeatedly as he attempts to move a couch up the stairs with fellow *Friends* Rachel and Chandler.

Picture yourself as a surfer, riding the waves out in the vast ocean. The waves are ever-changing—some are manageable, while others are downright gnarly. Just like surfing, life and business are full of waves, too. To succeed, you have to be flexible and adaptable. Sometimes, you'll have to roll up your sleeves and get your hands dirty. And when the moment comes, you'll need to pivot and change direction to ride the next wave to success.

One of the most important tools in your arsenal for navigating these waves is the power of the pivot. A pivot is a strategic shift in direction, and it can be a game-changer for your business or career.

Here are a few examples of well-known businesses that have pivoted over the years.

YouTube: When YouTube was founded in 2005, it was a platform for sharing short, low-quality videos. However, as the popularity of online video grew, YouTube pivoted to focus on longer, higher-quality videos. Today, YouTube is the second-most popular website in the world and is home to a vast library of video content.

Twitter: When Twitter was first launched in 2006, it was a platform for sharing short, text-based updates at 140 characters each. However, as users began to share photos and videos more frequently, Twitter pivoted to allow for richer media content like GIFs, memes, links, and polls. Today, Twitter is a hub for news, entertainment, and social interaction, with more than 450 million monthly active users. (By the way, you can use up to 280 characters now, and the new owner renamed it "X." Big pivot!)

To truly harness the power of the pivot in your life and career, it's important to have a clear roadmap to guide you. Here are some steps to help you get started (with some examples).

Step One: Keep an Open Mind

To pivot effectively, it is essential to stay aware of what's happening in your industry and the world at large. Keeping an open mind allows you to be receptive to new ideas and opportunities.

Stay curious and up-to-date with trends, apps, news, and developments in your field. Attend conferences, read industry publications, network with other professionals, and follow thought leaders in your industry on social media.

For example, here's how a social media marketer might stay aware of trends and developments to help their business.

If you notice that video content is becoming increasingly popular on social media platforms, you might pivot your business strategy to focus more on video production and distribution. You might attend conferences or workshops to learn about the latest video marketing techniques and network with other professionals in the field to stay on top of new developments.

Similarly, if you notice that a new social media platform is gaining popularity, you might pivot your business strategy to focus more on that platform. You might create new service offerings specifically tailored to that platform or hire new team members with expertise in using that platform to help your clients achieve their marketing goals.

Step Two: Evaluate Yourself and Your Current Strategy

Take a close look at your current business or career strategy. Are you achieving your desired results? What has worked well for you, and what hasn't? Are there any new technologies or market trends that you need to consider? Be honest with yourself and identify areas for improvement. Evaluate your strengths, weaknesses, opportunities, and threats (what's called a SWOT analysis) and consider how you can leverage your strengths and opportunities while mitigating your threats and weaknesses.

Here's an example of how a new, upcoming musician might evaluate her career strategy.

Strengths: A unique and recognizable voice, a well-developed stage presence, strong songwriting skills, and a loyal fanbase

Weaknesses: Limited resources and funding for recording and touring, difficulty standing out in a crowded industry, and a lack of connections within the music industry

Opportunities: The growing popularity of live streaming and virtual concerts, collaborations with other artists or producers, leveraging social media and digital marketing to reach a wider audience, and exploring new genres or styles

Threats: Intense competition from other artists, changing industry standards and trends, economic downturns, and the risk of being overshadowed by larger, more established artists

Based on this SWOT analysis, the singer might pivot her strategy to focus on leveraging social media and digital marketing to grow their fanbase and increase their visibility. She might also explore collaborations with other artists or producers to create new and innovative music and consider experimenting with new genres or styles to stand out in a crowded industry. To mitigate her weaknesses, she could investigate networking events, reach out to influencers or industry contacts, and seek out new sources of funding for recording and touring. Additionally, she might consider capitalizing on the growing trend of live streaming and virtual concerts to connect with fans and expand her reach beyond traditional performance venues.

Step Three: Test It Out

Here's an example of how testing and refining ideas can help a café pivot effectively.

As the owner of a café, you might consider pivoting your menu to focus on healthier, plant-based options in response to changing consumer preferences. Before committing fully to this change, it's essential to test your ideas to see how they resonate with your target audience.

First, find out if there's a demand in your area for plant-based options. You can survey your customers to gather feedback on their current eating habits and preferences and what they would like to see on your menu.

Next, you can invite some loyal customers to your café to test potential menu items and gather more detailed feedback. This can help you identify which plant-based options are the most popular, what price points are reasonable, and which ingredients and flavors are most appealing.

Based on this feedback, you might launch a small-scale pilot project to test your new menu items in a controlled environment. This could involve offering a limited selection of plant-based options for a short period of time and gathering feedback from customers who try them.

By using the feedback you receive, you can refine your ideas and make any necessary adjustments. For example, you might adjust your menu to include more—or less—of certain ingredients, change your pricing strategy, or rework your marketing messaging to better appeal to your target audience.

By testing and refining your ideas before committing fully to a pivot, you can increase the chance of success and ensure that your business remains competitive and responsive to changing consumer preferences. Don't be afraid to pivot again as needed, based on the feedback you receive from your customers.

Step Four: Take the Leap and Do It (And Repeat if Necessary)

Once you've identified a promising new direction, develop a detailed plan for how you'll make the transition. Communicate your pivot to your customers and fans and get everyone on board. Develop a timeline, a budget, and metrics to measure your success. Be prepared to make further adjustments along the way as you gather more information and feedback. Remember that pivoting is an ongoing process, and don't be afraid to pivot again if you need to.

Personal Sidenote

When I began my journey as a professional photographer, my services spanned a wide range of categories, including family portraits, infant photography, maternity shoots, wedding photography, event coverage, and corporate headshots. However, I realized that to stay ahead of the curve and align my business with my core values and mission, I needed to pivot and focus on a more specific niche: headshots and brand photography.

Through market research and conversations with colleagues and clients, I identified a growing demand for headshots and brand photography, particularly among professionals and entrepreneurs. I saw this as an opportunity to differentiate myself from other photographers and establish myself as the go-to resource for headshots and brand photography in my local market.

To effectively pivot my business strategy, I evaluated my current business and identified the areas where I was experiencing the most success (headshots and brand photography), as well as areas where I was struggling to differentiate myself from other photographers (weddings). Next, I identified a promising new direction and developed a detailed plan for how I would make the transition.

I communicated this change to my clients, social media followers, and industry contacts. I developed a detailed timeline for how I would make the transition, gradually phasing out my current services while building up my new niche through targeted marketing campaigns, networking events, and social media outreach.

Then I took the leap. With my mission, vision, and values in mind, I knew I would be able to build great rapport with my clients in a short amount of time by doing headshots and brand photography.

Most clients come into my studio a little shy and on edge, and they verbalize their dread of taking a photo. By the end of the session, I am confident they will walk out feeling energized, inspired, motivated, and ready to take on the world.

Overall, pivoting my business was a challenging but rewarding experience. By staying aware of market trends, gathering feedback from my target audience, developing a detailed plan, and sticking to what I loved, I was able to successfully differentiate myself from other photographers and set myself up for long-term success in my new niche. Now, I travel all over the country, meeting new people and capturing their stories through my lens. I am constantly refining my craft and pushing the boundaries of what's possible, always striving to deliver the best possible results for my clients. Whether it's a new entrepreneur looking to make a splash in her industry, or a seasoned professional looking to refresh his image, I am honored to be able to help my clients achieve their goals and tell their stories through stunning, eye-catching headshots.

By following some of these steps, you can harness the power of the pivot to stay ahead of the curve, identify new opportunities, and succeed in today's rapidly changing world. Keep an open mind, evaluate your strategy, identify new opportunities, test and refine your ideas, and execute as needed. With the right mindset, approach, and guidance, you can unlock your full potential and live a life of purpose and fulfillment.

Q

QUIT "SHOULD-ING" YOURSELF

"'Should' feels like too tight tube socks, cutting off circulation and causing all the uncomfortable itches."—Sarah Rainwater

———

As you move toward self-discovery and personal growth, one of the most difficult obstacles you might have to overcome is the habit of "should-ing" yourself. I hear it all the time: "I should have done this" or "I should be doing that." Ugh! This type of thinking is indicative of a fixed mindset—one that is focused on what a person thinks she should be doing rather than what she truly wants to do or feels is best for her.

Why do we "should" ourselves in the first place?

The act of "should-ing" yourself typically stems from two primary sources.

Fear and external factors: Society, culture, family, and friends can exert significant pressure on you to conform to certain ideals and standards. We internalize these expectations and measure our self-worth based on how well we adhere to them. The constant comparison and the fear of judgment can lead to a persistent feeling of not being good enough, triggering self-criticism and a barrage of "shoulds."

Internalized beliefs: Our own beliefs, often rooted in past experiences, can also contribute to the habit of "should-ing." These internalized beliefs dictate how we perceive ourselves and what we believe we should be doing. They can be a result of conditioning, past failures, or societal conditioning that has shaped our perception of success and happiness.

Examples of "Should-ing" Yourself

Career-related "shoulds": You might find yourself caught in a cycle of self-judgment when it comes to your career choices. For instance, you might think, "I should have pursued a more lucrative career," or "I should be in a higher position by now." These thoughts can arise from societal expectations or from comparing your progress to others, disregarding your individual aspirations and passions.

Relationship "shoulds": In relationships, people often place unrealistic expectations on themselves. For instance, you might think, "I should be married by now," or "I should have found my soulmate already." These "shoulds" can create feelings of pressure and anxiety, causing you to compare your love life to societal norms or the relationships of others. They can overshadow the genuine connections and personal growth that can be found in relationships that unfold naturally and authentically.

Procrastination: It's easy to take the future for granted and assume that we have all the time in the world to pursue our dreams and goals. However, the truth is that we never know what tomorrow will bring. There are no guarantees or promises that we will have another day, another opportunity, or another chance to make the most of our time here on Earth. This realization can be both humbling and empowering. It reminds us that every moment is precious and that we must make the most of the time that we have. It encourages us to live in the present moment, to savor every experience, and to cherish the people in our lives. It also challenges us to pursue our dreams and goals with passion and purpose, knowing that we might not have another chance to do so.

How can you stop should-ing yourself?

- Start by becoming aware of your self-talk and thought patterns. Pay attention to situations when you catch yourself using the word "should." Reflect on the underlying beliefs and expectations driving those thoughts.
- Question the validity and origin of your "shoulds." Are they truly aligned with your values, desires, and aspirations? Challenge societal norms and external expectations that might not serve your personal growth and happiness.
- Replace self-judgment with self-compassion. Treat yourself with kindness and understanding, just as you would a close friend. Understand that everyone has their own unique path and that mistakes and setbacks are part of the learning process.
- Take the time to define what success means to you personally. Identify your values, passions, and long-term goals. Focus on aligning your actions with your authentic self rather than meeting external expectations.
- Take inspired, intrinsically motivated action rather than becoming trapped in a cycle of "shoulds." Explore your passions, set realistic goals, and take steps toward living a life that feels meaningful and fulfilling to you.

The act of "should-ing" yourself often stems from fear and the influence of societal norms, but it doesn't have to define your path. Embrace inspired action, driven by your own motivation rather than external pressures. You will open up a world of possibilities and allow yourself to live authentically, with a sense of purpose and fulfillment. Your journey is unique, and it's up to you to define and pursue what truly matters to you. Let go of the "shoulds" and embrace the freedom to create a life that reflects your true desires and aspirations.

Success Story: From Flower Lover to Business Owner

Let's meet Charley, a woman with a profound love for flowers and a dream of opening her own shop. However, she often "should-ed" all over herself, thinking that she should pursue a more traditional career path and that her passion for flowers was merely a hobby. These self-imposed expectations prevented her from embracing her true calling.

One day, Charley decided to take a leap of faith and pursue her dream. She opened a charming flower shop in her town called the Paper Bag Bouquet, where she carefully curated a stunning collection of blooms and created unique arrangements. Little did she know that her signature touch, simple brown paper bag bouquets, would become a sensation.

Charley's talent and creativity were not confined to her shop alone. She also had a keen eye for capturing the beauty of her bouquets through photography. She began sharing her floral creations on Instagram, where her simple brown paper bag bouquets caught the attention of flower enthusiasts all over the world.

As Charley's Instagram following grew, her reputation as a talented florist spread like wildfire. Her photos inspired others to appreciate the beauty of simplicity and to find joy in the small things. Soon, she became an IG sensation, with thousands of followers eagerly awaiting her next floral masterpiece. She started shipping her products all over the country.

Embracing her newfound fame, Charley continued to expand her flower shop's offerings. She introduced workshops where she taught others her techniques for creating stunning yet understated arrangements. Her flower shop became a gathering place for flower lovers, both locally and from afar, who sought out her expertise and wanted to experience the magic of her brown paper bag bouquets firsthand.

Charley's success brought fulfillment and joy to her own life and also allowed her to share her passion with a broader audience. She proved that following one's true passion, even in a seemingly traditional industry, can lead to unexpected, remarkable outcomes.

Let Charley's story inspire you to break free from "shoulds," follow your passions, and create a life that is true to yourself. Embrace the beauty of simplicity, the power of your unique talents, and the limitless opportunities that await you on your own journey. You have the ability to turn your dreams into reality and make a meaningful impact in your own way.

R

REWARDS FOR YOURSELF AND OTHERS

"There is more hunger for love and appreciation in this world than for bread."
—*Mother Teresa*

———

In this chapter, we'll explore the importance of celebrating our own accomplishments (big and small) and those of others. We'll talk about ways to reward yourself and others that inspire growth, foster meaningful connections, and create an environment that motivates us to continue working toward our goals.

We often get caught up in the daily grind of life, focusing on what we need to do next instead of taking the time to celebrate our successes (or the successes of others). With the rise of digital communication and social media, traditional forms of expressing gratitude, such as sending handwritten thank you notes or small tokens of appreciation, have become less common.

Instead, we often express our appreciation through social media platforms, publicly acknowledge our achievements or expressing gratitude to others by tagging them in posts or sharing photos and videos of our experiences together. And while social media allows us to express our gratitude instantly, it can also feel impersonal and lacking in depth. A simple "like" or comment on a social media post doesn't carry the same weight.

Rewarding Ourselves

How do we reward ourselves? Identify what we want to celebrate. It could be a project you completed at work, a personal goal you achieved, finishing a chapter in your book, or something as simple as making it through a tough work week. Whatever it is, take the time to acknowledge and appreciate it. Then, find a way to reward yourself that aligns with your values and makes you feel good.

Here are some real-life examples of simple ways to reward yourself.

Take a break. If you've been working hard, take a break and do something you enjoy. It could be as simple as taking a walk in a park, reading a book, or watching a movie.

Treat yourself. Buy yourself something you've been wanting for a while, such as a new outfit, a fancy dinner, or a massage. Hit that weight loss goal? Buy those new shorts!

Take a trip or a long weekend. If you've been saving up, now's the time to put those plans in motion.

Learn something new. Sign up for a course or workshop about a subject or topic that interests you and you've been wanting to learn more about.

Rewarding yourself also has psychological benefits. It can help reduce stress, improve mood, and enhance overall well-being. Our brains release dopamine—a chemical linked to pleasure and reward —when we treat ourselves. This makes us feel good in the moment and also reinforces the behavior that led to the reward, making it more likely that we'll continue engaging in that behavior in the future.

It's also worth noting that rewarding oneself doesn't have to be limited to big accomplishments or milestones. In fact, rewarding oneself for everyday wins is just as important. Celebrating even the smallest successes can help us build momentum and stay motivated as we work toward our larger goals.

Rewarding (Celebrating) Others

Now that we've talked about how to reward ourselves, let's shift our focus to rewarding others. When we express our appreciation for others, it lets them know that they are valued. This can hold true for your family, your employees, a coworker, the teller at your local bank, your mechanic, the bus driver, or just about anyone.

Here are some examples of ways to reward others.

Give a compliment. Take the time to compliment someone on their work or something else that you appreciate about them. A sincere, thoughtful compliment can make someone feel seen, and it can help them see themselves in a more positive light. Be specific. If it's a coworker you're complimenting, maybe point out a specific point in their presentation that you found particularly insightful.

Do something thoughtful for someone. Surprising someone with a small gift or gesture, such as bringing them their favorite coffee or snack or treating them to lunch, can make them feel appreciated and seen.

Offer words of encouragement. Sometimes, all it takes to make someone's day is a few kind and supportive words. If you know someone who is going through a tough time or facing a challenge, take a few minutes to send them a message of encouragement or leave them a thoughtful note. Let them know that you believe in them and are there to support them.

Do a chore for someone. If you know someone who is feeling overwhelmed or stressed, offer to take a chore or task off their plate. It could be something as simple as doing their dishes or taking out the trash. This helps alleviate some of their stress and shows that you care, and that they're not alone.

Your Homework: The 30-Day Thank You Challenge

Are you ready to take the 30-Day Thank You Challenge? Imagine how it would feel to express gratitude and appreciation to someone every day for 30 straight days. I was challenged by my coach to do so, and I can tell you, it's a game changer. By participating in this challenge, you'll strengthen your relationships and cultivate a habit of giving thanks and gratitude that can have a positive impact on your mental and physical health.

Think about who you could thank. Maybe it's a family member, neighbor, mailperson, friend, coworker, a team member at Target, your local barista, or just someone who made your day a little brighter. Whoever it is, take the time to write a heartfelt note once a day for the next 30 days, expressing your gratitude for their help, support, or kindness. Reward them with your words.

A handwritten thank you note is a tangible, visible reminder of your gratitude that the recipient can keep and cherish. To aid in this challenge, I always keep a small box of blank cards, stickers, and fun pens on my desk. I even keep a few in my bag when I'm on the go so I'm always ready.

The 30-day Thank You Challenge is a small but powerful way to make a big impact in your life and the lives of those around you

Take the time to celebrate your accomplishments—big and small— as well as to express gratitude to others and watch as your relationships and personal growth thrive.

S

SHARING YOUR STORY

"Share your story with someone. You never know how one sentence of your life story could inspire someone to rewrite their own."—Demi Lovato

Sharing your story can be a game-changer when it comes to building meaningful connections with others. You might have heard the old sales adage that people buy from those they know, like, and trust. Telling your story is a powerful way to build that trust. When you let your guard down, open up, and show your vulnerability, you create a space for others to relate to you on a deeper level. Sharing your story can help you develop your personal brand, connect with others, and inspire positive change.

Telling your story can be therapeutic for you as well because each time you tell it, you gain a better understanding and acceptance of yourself. This takes courage and vulnerability. Letting people know the real you—not the one they've constructed for themselves—it leaves you in control of the narrative. After all, it is yours and yours alone.

You might think to yourself:

How much should I share?

What's the goal of sharing my story?

Is my story even worth telling?

Yes, your story is worth telling.

Here are some of the benefits to sharing your story.

Strengthen relationships and trust: Sharing a personal story with people can help them feel more connected and trustworthy. After hearing your story, people are more likely to identify with you personally and feel a stronger sense of connection. They might even want to ask questions and share their own experiences with you.

Promote positive change: Your story has the power to change people's lives and motivate others. By sharing your experiences, you can motivate people to take action, make changes in *their* lives, and work toward *their own* goals. Maybe hearing your story will encourage someone to take the leap and start their own business. You never know who is listening.

Create your own personal brand: Sharing your personal experience can help you develop your own brand. It can help you attract new clients or customers, establish yourself as an authority in your field, and build a following. No one else has your story. You are unique. Telling your story will make you stand out and be distinctively different.

Telling your personal story can be a powerful tool for self-reflection and increasing self-awareness. As you craft your narrative, take time to reflect on your experiences, values, and beliefs, staying true to yourself and your unique perspective. By exploring your personal story, you can gain a deeper understanding of yourself.

Establishing Boundaries

When sharing your personal story, it's important to respect your own boundaries. While it's important to be authentic and genuine, your feelings come first. The most important factor in deciding how much to share is your comfort level. You will become much more aware of your own feelings before you share them. If there are stories or memories that are too painful or that produce anxiety, you can choose not to share them at this time. You are the narrator of this story; you have control. When you are ready to share, you will find people ready to listen.

Your Audience

Consider who your audience is and what they're interested in hearing. If you're sharing your story in a professional setting, like a job interview or a sales pitch, you might want to highlight and talk about some success stories or ways you handled confrontation or a difficult situation at work.

On the other hand, if you're sharing your story with close friends or family members, you might feel comfortable sharing more personal details. You could open up about a personal challenge you've faced, such as dealing with a mental health issue.

What's the goal of telling my story?

You might have stories that are uplifting, empowering, and motivational. If you share some challenges you have faced and how you overcame them, as well as the lessons you learned, you may be helping others find hope and inspiration in similar circumstances.

You want to build trust. You could focus on the more vulnerable, personal details of your story. This will help your audience feel more connected to you and have some empathy. This will help develop that closer bond. Share your mistakes, too. For example, you might talk about a time when you felt overwhelmed and burned out and how you learned to prioritize self-care and set better boundaries in your personal and professional lives. This will help people see that you are real, rather than just a faceless brand or business.

You simply want to connect. You might share a story about how you coped with a particularly difficult flare-up of an illness. You could talk about the emotional toll it took on you and your family, as well as the physical pain and limitations you experienced. You might also share the strategies you used to manage your symptoms and get through the difficult period, such as meditation, gentle movement, or working with a healthcare provider. This will paint a more relatable portrait of yourself and give your audience a better understanding of who you are as a person.

While sharing personal details can be a powerful way to build trust and connection, it's important to balance that with respect for your own privacy and boundaries. By being intentional and thoughtful in what you choose to share, you can create a more meaningful, impactful conversation.

Someone is out there waiting for you to tell your story; are you ready?

———

Personal Sidenote

When I was born, I was named after my mom, Elaine. Growing up, to differentiate us from each other, I was called Lainey. No one called me Elaine. That was my mom. I kind of felt like the name was old-fashioned, so I preferred the nickname.

I grew up in a town called Willingboro, NJ. (Home to the Carl Lewis Stadium), I was a feisty little girl. I used to break dance, play kick-the-can, hide-and-seek, double-Dutch (I even broke my foot in seventh grade doing so!), play the violin, take Latin, play softball, and was also a pom-pom girl. I was well-rounded and always involved in something.

When I was five years old, my dad had a massive heart attack at age 52, and he immediately retired. (He was 47 when I was born.) My mom was a stay-at-home mom and had full-blown Systemic Lupus Erythematosus and was sick most of her life. Basically, I had both of my parents at home my entire childhood. Every day.

And I hated it at times.

I grew up in a very strict Italian household. My dad was 20 years older than my mom, so basically, it was like having multiple generations raise me. "No" in Italian meant the same in English, and I heard it a lot.

Can I go to a sleepover? No.

Can I stay out till 10 pm instead of 9 pm? No.

Everyone has new Jordache jeans, can I get a pair? No. (Can't afford them.)

Can I play in my room instead of drying the dishes? No.

Can I have a boyfriend? Hell No. (That one came from my dad and two older brothers.)

You get the picture.

Something clicked when I was about twelve years old. I started to work and got some more responsibility. I realized that because I couldn't change my parents, I might as well embrace them. Even though I was super well-rounded and active in school, I spent a lot of time with my parents.

Days at home felt like school. I learned so much from my dad: woodworking in the garage, how to use all the tools in the toolbox, take apart a lawn mower, change my oil and tires, fix the chain on my bike, install a wall air-conditioner, use a manual camera, bet at the track ($2 to win, number 5, Philadelphia Park), be a jokester and laugh, and play bingo, poker, and craps.

I learned even more from my mom: how to cook, clean, crochet, knit, balance a checkbook, do laundry, iron, sew on a machine, bake pizzelles, make homemade macaroni and meatballs with gravy (not sauce), and be a good friend, sister, wife, and mother.

The most important thing I learned from both my parents was *how to love.*

My parents were my best friends and gave me all the tools I would need from a very young age that I would carry with me for the rest of my life; these were the tools I needed to succeed. Both of my parents passed away when I was a young mom. So when people ask me, "Elaine, what can't you do?" I really can't think of anything. I know that if I can't do something, I will figure it out. If I *really* can't do something, I'll find a mentor or a coach to help me. If I *really, really* can't do something, like play horseshoes, I just say, "Not my thing," and move on.

For the past few years, friends and colleagues had started introducing me as a serial entrepreneur, and it was not easy for me to hear at first. I didn't really understand why they would call me that. Now I get it. I was raised to be all that I can be, and I know my parents would be so proud of all my accomplishments over the past few decades.

I'm a mom, wife, sister, and friend. I have a psych/business degree and am a registered nurse. I am a headshot and brand photographer. I own a café with my husband. I love to run multiple side businesses. I am a speaker and motivator. I love to write. I work because I enjoy it.

I am Lainey, but you can call me Elaine. I love my name now!

T

THINK BIG

"If your thoughts are as tall as the height of your ceiling, you can't fly above your room."—Israelmore Ayivor

Do you have ambitious aspirations but struggle to transform them into reality? Are you tired of settling for mediocrity and yearning for the extraordinary? It's time to embrace a mindset of thinking big. By doing this, you can recognize your limitless potential and find the courage to achieve your goals, no matter how big they might seem.

Why Thinking Big Is Important

Thinking big expands your horizons and opens up new possibilities for your life. Your current situation or previous experiences are not constraints when you think big. Instead, you're focused on what's possible and what you can achieve if you put your mind to it.

Thinking big empowers you to overcome self-doubt and fear. When you set big goals, you may initially doubt your ability to achieve them. However, as you take action and make progress toward your goals, you'll build confidence and realize that you're capable of more than you ever thought possible.

How to Think Big

Now that you understand the importance of thinking big, let's explore some actionable steps for how to actually do it.

Set a big goal. The first step to thinking big is to set some goals that challenge and stretch you beyond your comfort zone. The bigger your goals, the more motivated and inspired you'll be to achieve them.

Here are some tips for setting big goals.

- Make them specific and measurable.
- Write them down and review them regularly.
- Set deadlines for achieving them.
- Break them down into smaller, achievable tasks.
- Share them with someone who will hold you accountable.

Example: Running a marathon

If you're someone who's never run more than a mile, setting a goal to run a marathon might seem intimidating. However, it's a big goal that can motivate and inspire you to take action.

To make this goal specific and measurable, you could set a goal to run a particular marathon, such as the Marine Corps Marathon. You could then break down the goal into smaller, achievable tasks, such as running a certain number of miles per week, gradually increasing your mileage, and participating in shorter races as you build up to the marathon.

Visualize your success. Visualization is a powerful tool for thinking big. It creates a clear mental picture of what things will feel like when you've achieved your goals. This helps you stay motivated and focused.

Here are some tips for visualization.

- Close your eyes and imagine the goal you wish to achieve. Be as vivid as possible, engaging all your senses.
- Visualize taking the steps to achieve your goals.
- Picture the obstacles you might face and how you'll overcome them.
- Practice this visualization every day, until it becomes second nature to you.

Example: Writing a book

If your goal is to write a book, visualize the steps you'll take to achieve your goal, such as researching your topic thoroughly, creating an outline, and writing consistently every day. You could also visualize overcoming any obstacles you might face, such as writer's block or negative feedback. Then, visualize yourself holding a copy of your published book, feeling proud and accomplished. Visualize yourself sitting at a bookstore, signing books for the long line of readers out the door!

Get out of your comfort zone. To think big, you need to be comfortable with discomfort. This is where the real growth happens.

Here are some tips for getting out of your comfort zone.

- Try something new every day, such as a new recipe or walking route.
- Take on challenges that scare you, such as an improv class.
- Embrace failure as a learning opportunity.
- Seek feedback and learn from it.

Example: Starting a side hustle

Let's say you've always wanted to start a side hustle (like selling your crochet), but you're not sure where to begin. You could start by researching different business ideas, reading articles or books about entrepreneurship, or listening to podcasts about small businesses. Take that first step and register your business name or create a website, even if it feels overwhelming or intimidating. Ask friends and family to check out your site and get feedback. Use that feedback to improve and grow your business. Recognize that not every idea will be a success, but every failure is an opportunity to learn and improve.

Understand that merely *thinking* big is not enough. The key is to break down your big goals into smaller, more achievable tasks and work toward them consistently.

Believe in yourself and have the courage to pursue your dreams, no matter how big they might seem. It's about setting some goals, visualizing your success, expanding your comfort zone, surrounding yourself with positive influences, and taking action.

———

Personal Sidenote

I'm a firm believer in thinking big and pushing the limits of what's possible rather than settling for the status quo. Whether it's starting a new business venture, taking on a challenging project, or simply trying something new, I'm always eager to take on the next big thing.

What sets me apart is my willingness to embrace my identity as an ampersand. I'm not *just* a photographer. *Just* a café owner. *Just* a DIY enthusiast. I'm all of those things *and* more.

Being an *and* means that I'm constantly looking for ways to expand my horizons, try new things, and challenge myself. Personally, I'm not content with limiting myself to one identity or one passion. Instead, I'm always seeking out new opportunities to grow, learn, and evolve.

On the flipside, it's equally important to respect and support people who choose to embrace being a "just." There is beauty in mastering a single craft, dedicating oneself wholeheartedly to a singular pursuit, and finding immense satisfaction in doing so. We need individuals who excel in their chosen fields because they too contribute to the progress and advancement of society.

It's most important to be true to yourself, whether you resonate with being an "and" or a "just." Embrace your passions, explore new opportunities, and never be afraid to step outside the confines of what others deem possible. Success lies in finding your own path and embracing the journey with authenticity, passion, and purpose.

U

UNCOVERING YOUR WHY

"Believe in your infinite potential. Your only limitations are those you set upon yourself."—Anonymous

In this chapter, we'll uncover the hidden potential that lies within you. You might have heard the question, "What is your why?" Here, we will take a refreshing, unconventional approach to help you find your unique potential, whether you're starting a business, venturing into entrepreneurship, or simply seeking meaning in your daily endeavors.

Imagine walking into a busy marketplace filled with vendors selling the same product; let's use soap as an example. They all have the same features and benefits, the same quantity of products, and the same size kiosk, yet one vendor stands out from the crowd.

At this kiosk, there's a poster of a little boy with a huge smile on his face and soap bubbles on his cheeks.

When you approach this kiosk, you notice that instead of just listing the ingredients and benefits of the soaps for sale, this husband-and-wife duo shares the story of how their passion for natural skincare developed after their son experienced severe skin sensitivities. Their personal struggle—combined with their dedication to crafting gentle, chemical-free soaps—resonates with customers who seek similar solutions. It has *all the feels*. This engaging narrative—their story, their passion, and their purpose—is their no-longer-hidden potential that sets them apart from other vendors, making them relatable and creating a loyal customer base.

Uncovering your hidden potential or your "why" is about discovering your story, learning how to tell it, and connecting it to your work, and in turn, creating a compelling narrative that resonates with others. You already learned the importance of sharing your story in Chapter S, but now you'll uncover how to build that story. Your story.

The Story of You

Your journey, experiences, and unique perspective shape the person you are today. Reflecting on the moments in your life that have left a lasting impact is a powerful starting point for understanding your *why*. These could be triumphs, challenges, or instances that ignited a spark within you. Start writing them all down. By diving into the significance of these experiences, you uncover the core values, beliefs, and aspirations that have shaped you. Whether it's overcoming adversity, achieving personal milestones, or discovering passions that evoke a sense of purpose, these moments provide valuable insights into what truly matters to you. Connecting the dots between these experiences, identifying recurring themes, and considering the impact on others allows you to unearth the foundations of your why, paving the way for a purpose-driven, fulfilling life.

Success Story

Let's look at Sarah, a young professional. She embarked on a journey of self-discovery to understand her why. Reflecting on her life, she realized that overcoming a challenging career setback (getting laid off from her job of twelve years) was one of the most significant moments that ignited her passion for personal growth and resilience. This realization led her to connect the dots with other impactful moments, identifying a recurring theme of helping others on their journey of growth. Motivated by her insights, Sarah became a catalyst for transformation, offering guidance and support to individuals facing setbacks and promoting work-life balance, self-care, and positive relationships as a coach and mentor. Her journey exemplifies how reflecting on impactful moments can uncover core values, beliefs, and aspirations, paving the way for a purpose-driven life dedicated to empowering others to overcome challenges and live fulfilling lives.

Tapping into Your Talents to Discover Your Hidden Potential

Meet John, a true example of the transformative power of passion and purpose. His love for technology was unmatched. He was constantly immersed in tech gadgets, devouring magazines and articles on the subject, and attending conferences. However, John's passion didn't stop at personal interest. He realized that he could make a difference by leveraging his programming skills to create innovative e-learning platforms, making education accessible to all. His passion became his job, empowering individuals worldwide and revolutionizing education. John's story inspires us to combine our passions with purpose, unlocking our potential to create meaningful impact in the world.

Taking Action

Once you've discovered the "why" behind your actions, it's important to let it guide you in uncovering your hidden potential. Here are some simple strategies.

Create a vision board. Visualize your potential by creating a vision board that represents your aspirations, values, and desired impact. Use images, quotes, and symbols that resonate with you. Place your vision board where you can see it daily, reminding you of your purpose and keeping you focused. (We'll explore this further in the next chapter.)

Set meaningful goals. Establish goals that align with your why. Ensure they are "smart"—specific, measurable, attainable, relevant, and time-bound. Break them down into actionable steps, celebrating milestones along the way. By connecting your goals to your purpose, you'll find greater motivation to achieve them.

Seek support. Surround yourself with like-minded people who share your passion and values. Engage in networking events, join online communities, or seek out mentors who can offer guidance and support. Collaborating with others who understand your journey can provide valuable insights and encouragement.

As we reach the end of this chapter, I want to highlight the recurring principles that will guide you on your journey toward unlocking your gifts and living with purpose.

- Find accountability partners.
- Set meaningful goals that align with your purpose.
- Take consistent action.
- Visualize.

These principles will serve as your compass, leading you toward a purpose-driven, fulfilling life. Embrace them, embody them, and watch as they transform you—your why. The path to unlocking your gifts and living with purpose is within your reach. Keep moving forward.

———

Personal Sidenote

I want to tell you about my daughter, Emily, an emerging entrepreneur, and marketing guru who has a story of resilience, determination, and triumph. For years, she found herself confined within the boundaries of a back brace, wearing it for 23 hours a day to combat the challenges posed by scoliosis. Despite the physical constraints, Emily's spirit remained unbroken. She refused to be defined by her condition but instead rose above it, embracing the belief that she was not broken, but merely bent.

Through the trials and tribulations of her journey, my daughter's spirit shone brightly. Emily faced the daily discomfort and limitations with courage, inspiring those around her with her perseverance. While others might have viewed the brace as a burden, Emily saw it as a symbol of strength and a testament to her determination to overcome adversity.

In Emily's college entrance essay, she eloquently expressed the transformative power of her experience. She wrote about the physical and emotional challenges she endured, the moments of doubt and frustration, and the unwavering support of loved ones that bolstered her along the way. Her words painted a vivid picture of her journey from vulnerability to empowerment, from uncertainty to belief in her own capabilities. She called her brace her "cape."

Emily emerged as a beacon of hope and inspiration. Her story is not merely one of overcoming scoliosis but a testament to the human spirit's capacity to rise above any challenge. She exemplifies the transformative power of perseverance, reminding all of us that our circumstances do not define us; but rather, it is our response to those circumstances that shapes our character.

This is Emily's story of uncovering her hidden potential. And I'm one proud mom.

V

VOLUNTEER

"As you grow older, you will discover that you have two hands—one for helping yourself, the other for helping others."—Audrey Hepburn

---

In this chapter, we'll talk about how volunteering influences personal and professional growth. We'll also explore the benefits, strategies, and empowerment that come from giving back to our communities and society at large. Let's go on a journey that connects integrity, dedication, and love with the art of volunteering.

Here are some questions to ask yourself when you consider volunteering.

- Why do I want to help others?
- What causes do I care deeply about?
- What are my interests?
- What skills do I have that I can share or teach?

The Power of Giving Back

Volunteering goes beyond simple charity or throwing coins in a jar. When you give your time, skills, and money without the expectation of anything in return, you become a force for good and leave a lasting mark on the world around you. In addition, when you do things that are in line with your values and your vision, you find a deep sense of satisfaction and meaning in what you're doing. This fulfillment results from knowing that you are actively contributing to causes that are larger than yourself, causing a ripple effect of positivity that reaches far and wide. As you engage in acts of generosity, you cultivate a sense of purpose that resonates with every part of your being, bringing harmony and alignment to your life's journey and to the world around you.

The Benefits of Volunteering

Cultivating a strong network: Volunteering is a great way to meet different kinds of people who want to make the world a better place. By working with people, groups, and community leaders who share your interests, you can foster meaningful relationships without expecting anything in return. These connections can contribute to your personal and professional development, offering valuable experiences and insights.

Professional development and skill enhancement: When you volunteer, you have the opportunity to grow professionally and improve your skills. As you lend your time and talents to different projects, you learn new skills and improve upon the ones you already have. Volunteering can also help you learn how to be a better leader, enhance your public speaking skills, and gain hands-on experience in certain areas, such as carpentry, electric, and plumbing.

Demonstrating integrity, dedication, and consistency: Volunteering regularly and with dedication shows possible employers, clients, and coworkers that you are dedicated and passionate about what you do. It shows that you want to make a difference in the world beyond your direct responsibilities. While holiday seasons often bring an increased focus on charitable activities, the true essence of volunteering lies in its year-round dedication. By volunteering all year, you can make sure that the areas and causes you care about will continue to be helped.

Consider these tips to make the most of your volunteer time.

Define your passion. Reflect on the causes or social problems that resonate with you. Find the places where you can help the most with your time and skills. Focusing on causes that you care about will make your volunteer work more important and satisfying. And it won't seem like "work" at all!

Do research and make connections. Research volunteer opportunities and organizations in your area that fit your values and interests. Get in touch with these groups, let them know you're interested, and ask about volunteer opportunities. Building relationships with the right groups is important if you want to help in a way that makes a difference.

Start small. Be realistic about how much time you can devote to volunteering and start with time commitments you can realistically handle. Starting small also enables you to build momentum and gradually increase your impact over time.

Call upon your professional skills. Think about the professional skill set you already possess and figure out how you can use it in the volunteer world. Leveraging your professional skills will help you make a more significant contribution while also enhancing your own professional growth.

Think about the following ways to make volunteering a regular part of your life.

Schedule your volunteer time. Set aside specific times in your schedule for volunteering. Treat them as important commitments, just like you would any other professional or personal responsibilities. By making volunteering a regular part of your schedule, you're making a commitment to give back on a regular basis.

Seek long-term engagements. Look for volunteer opportunities that allow for ongoing involvement rather than one-time events. Long-term engagements give you the opportunity to develop deeper connections, contribute more significantly, and witness the transformative effects your efforts will have over time.

Participate in employee volunteer programs. Many companies have employee volunteer programs that encourage and help their staff give back to the community. Check out programs like this at your workplace and use the tools and chances they give you. This helps you grow as a worker, and it also makes your company look like a more socially responsible business.

Volunteer with friends or coworkers. Ask your friends, coworkers, or teams to volunteer with you. By doing things as a group, you can build a sense of community, strengthen relationships, and have a bigger impact. It becomes a way for everyone to work together to make a change and spread a culture of giving in their social or professional circles.

Where can you volunteer?

- Local non-profits: Do some research to find local non-profits that share your values. These groups usually have a wide range of volunteer opportunities, like helping at food banks, shelters, mentoring programs, or environmental projects.
- In your community: Check with the local community centers, youth clubs, or senior centers in your area to see if they have volunteer opportunities. These organizations often require volunteers for tutoring, organizing events, providing companionship, or leading recreational activities.
- Hospitals/health care facilities: Many hospitals and health care facilities have volunteer programs where you can help in a variety of different ways like spending time with

patients, helping with administrative tasks, or assisting with fundraising events.

- Animal shelters/rescues: If you love animals, consider volunteering at an animal shelter/animal rescue. You can help take care of the animals, get them used to people, assist with adoption events, or even offer your professional skills, like photography or graphic design.
- Schools and education programs: You might be able to help teachers in the classroom, give kids extra help with their homework, help with after-school programs, or join mentorship programs.
- Environmental and conservation initiatives: Get involved in projects that aim to protect the environment, make it more sustainable, or help restore ecosystems. Look for groups in your area that organize tree planting events, beach cleanups, or attempts to protect wildlife.
- International volunteer programs: If you have the time and money—and enjoy traveling—international volunteer programs that let you help build communities in other countries might be a good fit. Research reputable groups that offer opportunities that match your interests, and make sure that volunteering is done in a responsible, ethical way that aligns with your values.
- Disaster relief and emergency response organizations: When there are natural disasters or other emergencies, many groups offer people the chance to help with relief efforts. Research local and national disaster relief organizations so that you can be prepared to help affected communities when needed.

Remember to thoroughly research each organization, its mission, and its values, and assess their reputation before committing to any volunteering opportunity. By finding the right fit, you can maximize your impact and create a meaningful volunteer experience aligned with your passions and skills.

Volunteering is a powerful endeavor that empowers individuals to unlock their potential, create connections, and live a purposeful life. Giving back regularly throughout the year helps you make a lasting difference for the causes you support. One kind act at a time, your deeds show that you want to make the world a better place. So, move forward with purpose, start change, and inspire others through the power of consistent volunteering.

W

WISHES AND VISIONS

"Vision without action is merely a dream. Action without vision just passes the time. Vision with action can change the world."—Joel A. Barker

---

As adults, it's not ideal to express our wishes to others without sounding a little childish. Deep down, we all have wishes—big dreams that make us giddy inside. We all "wish" things, like living an abundant life, having a great job, or losing those five pounds. Embracing and expressing our wishes is a powerful, positive practice that fuels our personal growth and brings joy into our lives.

Wishing allows us to tap into our innate sense of imagination and possibility. It ignites our passion, inspires us to aim higher, and nurtures the belief that anything is attainable. Wishes act as the seeds of our dreams, and by acknowledging them, we give ourselves permission to explore our deepest desires.

Wishes become tangible when we dare to bring them to the fore-front of our consciousness. They require clarity, intention, and a sense of purpose. Try crafting a wish list that can give shape and form to your dreams, inviting them to take root in your life.

Take a moment to reflect on your deepest wishes and desires.

- What stirs your soul?
- How do you envision your dream home?
- What qualities does your ideal partner have?
- What brings you a sense of joy and fulfillment?
- If you could travel anywhere in the world, where would you go?
- What kind of work would make you feel fulfilled and purposeful?
- How would you spend your days living your best life?
- What skills, knowledge, or experiences do you desire to learn or develop?
- What kind of physical, mental, and emotional state do you aspire to have?
- What causes, issues, or areas of service are meaningful to you?

Let your pen dance across the paper as you really dive deep into your imagination and declare to the *universe* the life you envision for yourself. Remember to think *big*.

It's one thing to wish, but how do those thoughts become things?

Through action.

Once you have clearly defined your wishes, it's time to align your actions with your aspirations. This involves taking steps, both big and small, toward the realization of your dreams.

For example, if your wish is to start a successful business aligned with your passion, take proactive measures to research, plan, and execute your ideas. Seek out mentors, acquire the necessary skills, and embrace a growth mindset. By consistently moving forward, you create momentum and open doors for opportunities to manifest.

Similarly, if you desire deep, fulfilling love, it's important to cultivate self-love and become the person you aspire to be. Engage in activities that bring you joy and personal growth and be open to meeting new people who align with your values. Nurture genuine connections and communicate your needs and desires openly, allowing love to flow into your life.

Now let's talk about visions. Wishes and visions are interconnected but different concepts. Wishes are desires or aspirations that reside within us, often reflecting our immediate wants or needs. They are typically based on external circumstances or outcomes we hope to achieve.

On the other hand, visions encompass a broader perspective. They involve a deep sense of purpose, values, and long-term goals that guide our actions and shape our lives. Visions are rooted in our core values, passions, and the overall direction we want our lives to take.

While wishes might focus on specific desires or material outcomes, visions encompass a holistic view of our ideal life, encompassing various aspects, such as relationships, personal growth, career, and contribution to society.

Take a look at the difference between a wish and a vision.

Wish: I wish to travel to Italy someday.

This wish expresses a desire to visit a specific location, but it is relatively specific and focused on a single event or experience.

Vision: I envision a life of adventure, where I travel the world, immerse myself in different cultures, and create unforgettable memories. One of my top destinations is Italy, where I can explore its charming streets, indulge in its cuisine, and experience its rich history and art.

This vision expands beyond a single wish and paints a broader picture of a lifestyle filled with travel, exploration, and personal growth. It covers a range of experiences, cultures, and destinations, with Italy being one of many desired travel experiences.

While the wish is more narrowly focused on a specific desire, the vision includes a deeper sense of purpose and a broader perspective on how travel contributes to a fulfilling, adventurous life.

Vision boards serve as powerful tools to support the manifestation of our visions and desires. They are visual representations of our goals, wishes, and aspirations. By creating a vision board, you help to bring your vision to life.

Vision boards typically consist of images, words, and symbols that represent the life we envision for ourselves. They help us clarify our desires, enhance our focus, and keep us motivated and inspired.

Here's a step-by-step guide on how to create a vision board:

Step One: Set Your Intentions

Take some time to reflect on your goals, aspirations, and the areas of your life you want to focus on. Clarify what you want to manifest and the feelings you want to experience. Before you start, take a few minutes to answer the following questions.

- What is one thing you always wanted to do but never had the courage to start?
- What quotes, images, or phrases come to mind when you envision reaching your goal?
- Who or what do you wish you had more time for in your life right now?
- If money or resources were not an issue, what would you be doing right now?
- If you could close your eyes right now, where would you like to wake up?

Step Two: Gather Materials

Collect magazines, stickers, newspapers, images, quotes, and any other visual elements that resonate with your intentions. You can also print images from the internet or use photographs. Additionally, you'll need a poster board, corkboard, or a digital platform to create your vision board.

Step Three: Visualize and Select Images

Flip through the materials you gathered and let your intuition guide you. Look for images and words that evoke positive emotions and represent the life you envision. Trust your inner voice and choose what resonates with you the most.

Step Four: Arrange and Create Your Board

Arrange the selected images and words on your poster board or digital platform. There are various ways to organize them—by theme, area of life, or simply based on what feels right to you. Get creative with the layout, using colors, patterns, and other decorative elements to make it visually appealing.

Step Five: Add Personal Touches

Enhance your vision board by adding personal touches such as photographs, drawings, or handwritten affirmations. These personalized elements bring a deeper sense of connection to your vision board.

Step Six: Reflect and Visualize

Once your vision board is complete, take a moment to sit with it. Place it where you can see it regularly—a prominent spot in your living space or as your digital wallpaper. (I keep mine on my phone as my background.) Spend time looking at it, visualizing yourself living the experiences depicted on the board, and connecting with the emotions associated with your desires.

Step Seven: Take Inspired Action

Your vision board serves as a powerful reminder of your intentions, but it's important to remember that it is not a magic solution. It's now time to take inspired action aligned with your desires. Use your vision board as a guidepost, taking steps toward your goals and making choices that support your vision.

————

Personal Sidenote

Every January 1ˢᵗ, I create my vision board for the year. A few years ago, I was thinking big, and put a picture of a Red Carpet on my vision board. (Along with a Jeep Grand Cherokee, a pile of money, a house on the May River in South Carolina, and the words *empower* and *inspire* all over it.) I had a photo of my finished board on my phone screensaver. In June of that year, I was invited, at the last minute, to the *Tony Awards* with my friend Kristine. We got all dolled up, and when we arrived, we got to walk on the Red Carpet in New York City! The Red Carpet! EEEEK! What a dream!

And as a bonus, I got to meet Josh Groban, Justin Guarini, Keegan-Michael Key, President Joe Biden, and First Lady Jill Biden. Oh, what a night! When I was going home the next day, I glanced down at my phone and realized the Red Carpet cut-out from my vision board was on my phone's screensaver. I was blown away. I showed my friend, and we were both amazed that it came true.

This story serves as a reminder that the power of vision boards and manifesting our desires is real and can lead to extraordinary experiences. I did get a Jeep eventually, but I don't have a pile of money, and I've yet to get a house on the May River. However, I do make sure I put that cute little house on my board every year.

As you create your own vision board, think big, be courageous, and trust in the magic of your wishes. Visualize the life you aspire to live, and let your board serve as a constant reminder of your intentions. Look at it from time to time and embrace the journey of manifestation, knowing that the universe has the power to align circumstances in your favor. Keep taking inspired action, stay open to fun and spontaneous opportunities, and watch as your dreams unfold before your eyes.

X

X-TRA MILE

"It's never crowded along the extra mile."—*Wayne Dyer*

In today's interconnected world, simply meeting the expectations of the people in our lives won't always set us apart from others. To truly stand out and nurture meaningful connections, we must go beyond the ordinary. By going the extra mile, even by just 1 percent more, we demonstrate an unwavering commitment to exceptional care and consideration and experience the transformative impact it has on our personal relationships.

A Simple, Thoughtful Gesture

One of the most impactful ways to exceed expectations in our personal connections is through thoughtful gestures that demonstrate genuine care and attention to detail. Even in a world where digital communication predominates, we've all experienced the power of a heartfelt handwritten note, as covered in the R chapter.

Surprise gestures are another powerful way to show our commitment to exceptional care. By surprising the people in our lives with unexpected acts of kindness (and they don't have to be grand or expensive), we can go beyond the norm and make them feel truly special. These personalized surprises contribute to fostering strong, lasting relationships because people feel a genuine connection with us. Let's explore four quick, easy examples of personalized surprises we can give to someone special in our life.

Customized care package: Create a personalized care package with items that align with their interests or needs, such as a favorite snack, a small token related to their hobbies, or a gift card to a local café.

Thoughtful treat: Surprise them with a small, thoughtful treat like a delicious cookie, a cup of their preferred coffee, or a homemade treat accompanied by a heartfelt note expressing your appreciation for them.

Personalized recommendation (free!): Provide a personalized recommendation, such as a movie, TV show, or podcast, that aligns with their interests or offers a solution to a challenge they've mentioned. It shows that you pay attention to their preferences and genuinely care about their well-being.

Exclusive access or discount: If you own a business, surprise them with exclusive access to an event or activity they would enjoy or provide them with a special discount or offer for something they need. It's about making them feel valued and showing that we go the extra mile to support them.

The key is to customize these surprises based on their preferences, interests, and needs. By going the extra mile with personalized gestures, you can foster meaningful connections and build a sense of trust and appreciation.

Quick Response Time

Swift, responsive communication is vital for going the extra mile in our personal connections. People value those who prioritize prompt communication and address their needs with efficiency. Responding to messages or calls within a reasonable time frame, even if you don't have all the answers immediately, shows your commitment to staying connected. Acknowledging their communication and providing a timeline for a complete response reassures them that you value their time and input. It's about going above and beyond to keep them engaged and to maintain a strong connection.

Exceptional Experiences

Creating exceptional experiences for the people in our lives is a powerful strategy to nurture lasting relationships and make a positive impact. Planning special outings, organizing surprise gatherings, or arranging meaningful activities tailored to their interests and preferences allows us to show our genuine care and make them feel truly seen and appreciated. These experiences create lasting memories and provide opportunities for us to deepen our connections and foster a sense of belonging.

Taking the time to listen attentively, providing thoughtful advice, or sharing resources that align with their goals or challenges shows that you go the extra mile to support their journey.

By embracing these strategies and going the x-tra mile in our personal connections, we can cultivate meaningful relationships, inspire trust, and create a positive impact in the lives of those around us.

Success Story

Kristine, an event planner and the founder of KLO-Events based in Easton, Pennsylvania, embodies the spirit of going above and beyond by forging deep connections with her clients on a personal level. She understands the importance of getting to know her clients better (even when the events are over) and goes the extra mile to maintain relationships beyond the professional realm. Through social media interactions, texting, attending local events, and organizing outings, Kristine creates opportunities to connect with her clients in meaningful ways.

Kristine is also very observant. She pays attention to posts, texts, and emails that mention events going on in her clients' lives. When it comes to celebrating milestones like births or weddings, Kristine's thoughtfulness shines through. She takes the time to select personalized gifts for her clients' loved ones, adding an extra touch of warmth and care to these joyous occasions. Likewise, during times of hardship, such as illnesses or family losses, Kristine extends her support by sending thoughtful care packages, flowers, or baskets. Her gestures of compassion provide comfort and reassurance to her clients during difficult times.

Kristine's dedication to fostering personal connections and her genuine concern for her clients' well-being exemplify her commitment to going above and beyond. By recognizing the significance of both joyful and challenging moments in her clients' lives, she demonstrates the true essence of exceptional service and client care. The connections she forms with her clients nourish her own sense of connection and purpose. Ultimately, for Kristine, her work is not just a job; it's a calling. It aligns with her values and allows her to make a meaningful difference in the lives of others.

———

Personal Sidenote

In my photography business, I love to sprinkle in a little extra something to provide an unforgettable experience for my clients. I don't just capture amazing, empowering headshots. I go the extra mile to create exceptional experiences that the client will cherish long after the shoot. Because my own personal mission is to help other people become more empowered, I make it a point to ensure that the time I spend with my clients reflects this goal, whether we are meeting for five minutes or for a full two-hour session. My objective is to make my client shine by providing a headshot that consistently demonstrates likeability, look-ability, connectivity, and empowerment. Every. Single. Time.

It's fascinating to observe that a staggering eight out of ten of my clients initially approach this experience as if it were an unwanted chore or even an annoyance of sorts. Most clients possess a natural shyness, and they tend to be excessively critical of their own appearance and how they view themselves.

Before we begin the shoot, I like to sit down and have a little chat with my clients. We'll share some laughs, talk about their vision and brand, and ensure they feel completely at ease because when they're comfortable and relaxed, that's when the real magic happens! It's so much more fun when we feel like old friends just enjoying a great time together. I get to see their genuine smile way before they step in front of my camera.

I know that letting your real self shine in front of a stranger's camera can be intimidating, so I've adopted a gentle, empathetic approach, assuring my clients that they are in a safe, judgment-free space. As our journey together progresses, I witness remarkable transformations taking place. The camera becomes a conduit for self-expression and self-discovery. With each click, my clients shed their inhibitions and embrace their unique beauty and individuality. They transcend their initial reservations and embrace the profound truth that they are worthy of admiration and appreciation.

It is an amazing honor to see my clients' confidence grow as they look at themselves through the mirror of my lens. They realize that they are so much more than their perceived flaws or limitations. They embrace their own unique qualities, quirks, and strengths, understanding that these are the very aspects that make them beautiful.

Bold.

Extraordinary.

Empowered.

I am their biggest cheerleader.

That's the x-tra I deliver.

Y

YOU GOT THIS!

"Authenticity is the shining star in a world of copycats and filters. Embrace your uniqueness, radiate magnetic energy, and watch as genuine connections bloom around you!"—Elaine Zelker

---

You've embarked on a remarkable journey of self-discovery, and now it's time to show the real *you* to the world. Let's look at ways to present yourself authentically, build self-esteem, and captivate others with a powerful elevator pitch! When you master the pitch, your confidence will skyrocket, and you'll be so proud of who you are and what you stand for that you'll want to share that with the world.

Embrace the Strength of Your True Self

A strong sense of self-esteem is the cornerstone of confidence. It forms a shatterproof foundation that shields us from the gusts of self-doubt. We must never dismiss the gentle inner voice that whispers, "You are capable, worthy, and deserving. You've got this." With strong self-esteem, we no longer seek external validation or approval. Instead, we cultivate positive self-talk that fuels our belief in our own abilities. We embrace our strengths and talents, banishing any traces of self-doubt. By revisiting the empowering "I am" statements from Chapter I, we reinforce our positive self-talk, fortifying our self-esteem, and unlocking boundless confidence within.

If you let the negativity in, your actions will suffer, your decision-making will become weak and clouded, and you will start to hesitate. You will freeze. You might begin to fear your dreams and aspirations are not good enough or deserving of success. You may find yourself trapped in a cycle of self-sabotage, unconsciously undermining your own potential.

Oh, heck no! You must nip that in the bud. You must regain control. It's time to reclaim your power and silence your inner critic. Embrace your worth and watch as your potential soars beyond the limits you once thought were insurmountable. You are deserving of success, and with unwavering determination, you will forge your own path to greatness.

In your quest for greatness, there's a crucial step you must take to overcome the barriers that hinder your progress. It all begins by *challenging your limiting beliefs* and reclaiming control of your mindset. Identify the negative beliefs that hold you back and challenge their validity. Change them up with empowering beliefs that support your growth and inner strength.

Limiting belief: I can't start my own business because I lack experience.

Empowering belief: I can gain the necessary skills and knowledge to start my own business through taking classes, seeking guidance from experts, and finding accountability partners.

Limiting belief: I can't speak in public because I am too shy.

Empowering belief: I can improve my public speaking skills through practice, preparation, and seeking opportunities to speak in front of others.

Limiting belief: I can't dance because I have two left feet.

Empowering belief: I can free my inner J.Lo. and jam out to the beat, embracing my unique style and having a blast on the dance floor! YOLO!

Here are some points to review.

Encourage self-reflection. Give yourself some time to consider your abilities, principles, interests, and special traits. Recognize the abilities, knowledge, and experiences that truly define your awesomeness. Celebrate your successes and the effects they have on other people.

Practice self-compassion. Be kind to yourself as you would a close friend when it comes to pointing out your shortcomings and blunders. Accept self-compassion as a means of cultivating a nurturing relationship with yourself.

Surround yourself with positive influences. Find friends, mentors, and role models who are upbeat and encouraging and who value and accept you for who you are. Participate in activities or organizations that value uniqueness and promote personal development.

Visualize your success. Use visualization techniques to picture yourself realizing your potential and succeeding. Consider the beneficial effects you can have on people and the environment. Your self-confidence will be strengthened by engaging in this practice.

Combat perfectionism and comparison. Don't fall into the pitfall of evaluating yourself against others. Keep in mind that every person has her own unique journey, and you have your own path to take. Allow yourself to be imperfect. Instead of pursuing an impossible ideal, place more emphasis on personal development and advancement.

Celebrate your accomplishments. No matter how minor, acknowledge and appreciate your successes. Recognize the time and effort you invested in achieving your objectives and value the advancements you have made.

Build a strong you and then send yourself out into the world! Believing in your authentic awesomeness is a journey, and it takes time and practice. Be patient with yourself and embrace the process of self-discovery and self-acceptance. Trust in your distinct, unique qualities and the positive impact you can make in the world. You are truly amazing, and the more you believe in it, the more it will shine through in everything you do.

Mastering the Elevator Pitch

Now that you've got the tools down and your cape on, it's time to present the authentic, confident, distinctively different, fearless, and empowered you to the world.

It's time to create your elevator pitch.

An elevator pitch is a short, impactful introduction (think 30 seconds) that helps you make a memorable first impression. It showcases your strengths, highlights your unique value, and creates opportunities by capturing the attention of others. It's a powerful tool for networking, forming relationships, and boosting your confidence. With a clear, concise elevator pitch, you can confidently communicate who you are and what you have to offer in a compelling way.

Scenario: Imagine stepping into an elevator with your ideal employer and having 30 seconds to make a lasting impression.

What would you say?

Before we break it down, let's look at some examples.

Before mastering the pitch.

"Um, hi. I'm Alex. I, uh, work in marketing, I guess. I have some experience with social media and stuff. Like, I'm not sure what makes me unique, but, uh, yeah, I'm here looking for opportunities."

After mastering the pitch:

"Hi, I'm Alex, a marketing professional specializing in social media strategy and campaign management. With a proven track record, I create compelling digital experiences that captivate audiences and elevate brands. I'm passionate about leveraging data-driven insights to optimize marketing efforts and maximize ROI. Let's connect and explore how I can help your organization achieve its marketing objectives and stand out in the digital landscape."

Before mastering the pitch:

"Hi, I'm Sam. I've worked in customer service and some administrative roles. I'm organized and good with people, I guess. Looking for new opportunities."

After mastering the pitch:

"Imagine having someone on your team who is incredible at making customers happy and really good at keeping things organized and running smoothly. Sound intriguing? Well, look no further! Hello, I'm Sam. With a background in customer service and administrative excellence, I possess a passion for delivering exceptional results. Let's connect and discuss how my skills in fostering customer satisfaction and optimizing workflows can contribute to the success of your team."

See the potential of a good elevator pitch?

Here are some tips on how to create one.

Start with a captivating hook. Begin your elevator pitch with a thought-provoking question or a captivating statement that grabs attention. For example: "Did you ever wonder how some brands effortlessly capture the attention of millions and create a spark that spreads like wildfire?"

Highlight your secret sauce. Identify your key strengths, talents, or accomplishments that set you apart. Remember, you are one-of-a-kind! For instance: "At our PR company, we are masters of storytelling and brand positioning. We craft compelling narratives that resonate with audiences and establish a lasting connection."

Connect emotionally. Appeal to the emotions of your audience by illustrating the impact and benefits of your skills. Paint a vivid picture of the positive outcomes your work can achieve. For example: "Imagine the impact of having your brand's story told in a way that evokes emotions, builds trust, and inspires action. Our expertise in strategic communication can help you achieve that."

End with a call to action. Conclude your elevator pitch by inviting further engagement or leaving a lasting impression. This could be a question or an invitation to connect. For instance: "Are you ready to take your brand to new heights? Let's schedule a meeting to discuss how our PR strategies can amplify your presence, engage your target audience, and drive exceptional results."

Here's another example (with a breakdown):

Meet Taylor, an aspiring entrepreneur who wants to confidently present herself to potential investors.

Taylor crafts her elevator pitch: "Are you seeking to invest in an innovative solution that will disrupt the healthcare industry? Look no further! I am the visionary behind a cutting-edge digital health platform that combines technology, accessibility, and personalized care. Let's explore how my passion for improving healthcare outcomes and my expertise in leveraging technology can drive us toward a healthier future."

You can hear Taylor's confidence. How did she get to this point?

- Taylor has high self-esteem.
- Taylor overcomes self-doubt by challenging the fear of rejection or failure.
- Taylor cultivates a positive self-image by highlighting her strengths and unique qualities.
- Taylor exudes confidence by attracting potential investors who share her vision for a better, more accessible future in healthcare.

I'd invest in Taylor!

And here's mine.

I'm Elaine Zelker, a photographer, serial entrepreneur, and passionate advocate for empowering others to rise and soar. With more than thirteen years of experience capturing the perfect headshot, I've had the pleasure of photographing countless individuals across the country. My mission goes beyond photography. My purpose is to help you tap into your unique gifts and talents, level up your craft, and build an abundant business. From guiding you in developing a powerful personal brand to providing expert insights and strategies, I'm here to support your journey of growth and success. Let's work together to unlock your full potential, embrace your true passion, and create a business that aligns with your values and aspirations.

Now, that's the formal, written one. I'd speak that way at a Toastmasters or other professional meeting. If I were to meet someone in an actual elevator, I'd say this.

"Hi, I'm Elaine Zelker; I'm a headshot photographer and serial entrepreneur with years of experience, and I'm all about empowering others to rise and soar by helping them level up their craft and build a thriving business. My goal is to help others develop their own mission, vision, and values and lead a life with purpose."

Embracing your authentic self, developing a compelling elevator pitch, boosting your self-esteem, overcoming self-doubt, and cultivating a positive self-image are all necessary for presenting yourself confidently to the world. Keep in mind that you are a unique person with your own talents and skills. You can confidently display your true potential to the world by highlighting your strengths, accepting your flaws, and engaging in the practice of self-compassion. You have all the tools in your arsenal to rock your elevator pitch with confidence and flair. So go forward, light up the world, and leave a mark with your genuine presence. It's time to show the world what you're made of!

Z

ZERO LIMITS

Dear Reader,

Congratulations on making it through this incredible journey of self-discovery, empowerment, and growth! I am beyond thrilled to be here with you as you reach the final chapter of this book. Throughout these pages, we have explored various aspects of personal and professional development, diving deep into topics that have the power to transform your life. Now, as we conclude our journey together, I want to remind you of *my* mission: **"To empower women to use their gifts and talents to rise and soar by helping them level up their craft and build an abundant life and business."**

Every word, every exercise, and every insight shared were designed to ignire a fire within you, reminding you of your unlimited potential, and empowering you to take inspired action.

As you embarked on this journey, we explored different strategies, tools, and mindsets to help you clarify and cultivate your own vision. I want you to dream big, think big, and create a compelling future that excites and motivates you to succeed. Keep in mind that circumstances or outside factors do not limit your vision. Rather, your vision reflects your heart's desires and the impact you wish to make in the world.

Throughout this book, I have emphasized the importance of values. Your values are the compass that guides your decisions, actions, and relationships. By staying true to your values, you align yourself with the authentic path that leads to fulfillment and success. As you rise and soar, never compromise your values. They are the core of who you are and what you stand for.

One crucial element can propel you even further on your journey: stepping outside your comfort zone. Comfort zones can be cozy and familiar, but they can also be limiting. When you dare to step outside your comfort zone, you open yourself up to new experiences, opportunities, and growth. In those moments of discomfort and stretching, you discover your true potential and achieve breakthroughs you never thought possible. Embrace the discomfort as a sign of growth and progress.

As you venture into uncharted territories, remember that you are not alone. You have the knowledge, tools, and support to guide you. The chapters in this book have provided you with strategies and insights to overcome fear, embrace change, and develop the courage to take bold action. Trust in yourself and in the process.

You now know the importance of having accountability partners, being fearless, and being distinctively different. You now know how you can learn to *love yourself* first and ways to give back, give thanks, and practice gratitude. You now know the importance of *joy* in your life and how that can inspire you to try new things and create new habits. You can now create your own mission statement and build an amazing elevator pitch utilizing your own personal story. It's all here.

Zero limits: That's what this book is all about. It's about breaking the boundaries that hold you back. It's about challenging the self-imposed limitations that keep you from reaching your full potential. When you embrace the concept of Zero Limits, you tap into the infinite power that resides within you. You realize that your potential is boundless and that you can achieve anything you set your mind to. The path to greatness lies beyond what is comfortable and familiar.

Now, spread your wings, soar to new heights, and show the world what you are truly capable of. The power to create the life of your dreams lies within you. Embrace your story, live your vision, honor your values, and let the concept of Zero Limits guide your every step.

I am honored to have been your guide—and your biggest cheer-leader—on this journey, and I cannot wait to witness the incredible heights you will reach. Share your successes, wins, or obstacles by reaching out to me at info@elainezelker.com.

Believe in yourself, trust in your abilities, and embrace the adventure that awaits.

Rise and soar,

Elaine

Acknowledgments

What started seven years ago as *The EZ Method: A-Z* has morphed into *Zero Limits*, but not without some sweat, tears, and lots of support. I have so many to thank.

First, to Zeke and "the girls," thank you for giving me the time and space to "be me."

To those who have taken my workshop in the past: Keep on keeping on! Remember when I told you that there would come a time when you had to take fear, squash it, and go for it? I went for it, and *you* can, too! I look forward to pouring into so many more people.

To my photography clients, Thank you for allowing me to do what I love, capture your true essence, and create a space for you to let your guard down and be you.

To my pre-launch readers: Emily Campbell, Corrine Kavounas, Tina Joynes, Kathy Fleming, and Jesse Damiano, thank you for taking the time to give me your feedback, critique, and words of encouragement.

To Christine Krahling, my editor, thank you for your skills, for believing in this project, and for being an early cheerleader.

To Jennifer Bright (Bright Communications), my publisher. Thank you for being a fan from day one. Thank you for your service. Thank you for being there for me when I doubted and thank you for hearing me when I wanted it to be "just right."

Thank you for being a friend and sounding board to: Bob DiBella, Barbara Scullion, Kristine Ortiz, Lori Kantor, "My CEO Group:

Ashley, Tina, Lenore, Maria, Virginia, Katie," Jill Fritzo, the Zekraft Team, and the fabulous Lehigh Valley, PA. Also, to Danelle Delgado, my first and best coach, thank you for pouring into me the way you did. It's working!

About the Author

In addition to her new love for writing, Elaine has been running her photography business in the Lehigh Valley, PA, since 2010. She has mastered the "perfect headshot" and has enjoyed photographing thousands of people all over the country.

Known as a serial entrepreneur, Elaine has multiple side hustles and businesses. She's a mom, an RN, a photographer, café owner, brand strategist, wife, social retailer, author, DIYer, speaker, and lover of life!

She has three amazing daughters (and three pups), and lives in Easton, PA with her husband, Zeke.

"My mission is to empower others to use their gifts and talents to rise and soar by helping them level up their craft and build an abundant business."
—*Elaine Zelker*

Connect

Looking for my one-on-one professional mentoring series? Contact me at info@elainezelker.com or www.elainezelker.com/brandingandmentoring for more information.

Made in the USA
Middletown, DE
22 March 2024

51493197R00091